Rescued by the Coastguard - My Journey of Bouncing Back

NICKY MARSHALL

ISBN: 099567860X

ISBN-13: 9780995678606

DEDICATION

This book, as always, is dedicated to my amazing family and friends. I am blessed to know so many awesome people! Thank you for the support, the love, the raised eyebrows and the gentle nudges that have given me the courage and confidence to step out into the world of making a difference. My hope is that your life is a better place as a result of me, as mine is because of you.

TABLE OF CONTENTS

FOREWORD

By Marsha Wright ~ Entrepreneur, TV Business Expert, #1 Best Selling Author and Media Personality
Twitter: @MarshaWright

The road to happiness and fulfilment is a winding one for us all. On that journey we all have niggly doubts we'll make it, we experience things that throw us completely. But somewhere on that path—that nature and nurture have defined—if we're lucky, we experience a little glint of magic that signals to us that we can not only survive, but thrive and do something truly magical.

In Rescued by the Coastguard, My Journey of Bouncing Back, Nicky Marshall takes us on an unveiling of our story… yes it's in her words, it draws on her story… But while I read her book, I kept seeing more of me in what she wrote. While reading she spoke to the me that doesn't put myself first enough at times. Do you have the same tendency? The you that wants to be reliable and never let others down. The you that knows something spectacular and out of this world is irking to burst free if you'll let it. I believe, while getting lost in Nicky's world, that you can give yourself permission to expand your potential by going for it - every day of your life.

Bravery, courage and boldness are always within us… even if we've a quiet and unassuming personality. On the winding journey that this book provides, you'll feel so close to Nicky's story because she is you, she is us. She is every woman and man who takes on far too much, anxious to fulfil their purpose and please. She is the person you can always count on, and that resonated with me so much because in the pursuit of being 'there' for everyone else, she did what so many of us do… we often sabotage ourselves, being reliable for everyone else.

If you've been looking for permission to dig deep and *discover your bounce-back,* then this book is a wonderfully touching passport from here to there.

When Nicky asked me to do this foreword, it was an easy yes for me. I have come to know Nicky very well following a magical six months taking her under my wing. I remember the chat we had that acted as the springboard. Nicky knows she is able to impact the world, and it's her passion, it's what drives her. I'm sure you'll enjoy this book and see how her successful journey to get her *bounce* back, can encourage you to re-discover your inner power and do the same.

ACT ONE

INTRODUCTION

I wondered if the figure waving from the jetty thought it was a mistake too? I had put on a brave face and a big smile, reassuring my husband Phil that of course I should go to hospital alone, why should his diving be interrupted and anyway, who else would pack up our camping and diving kit? That fierce independent streak of mine had raised its head and now it was too late to go back.

Logically of course my decision made perfect sense. Perfect logic. I knew how much Phil loved to dive, but I realised now that perhaps he would have liked to be with me, to hold my hand and tell me everything would be okay…and perhaps I would like that too. Would he enjoy the diving at all until he knew I was better? There was no ferry until the following afternoon and so our decision couldn't be undone. I reasoned I would get checked out and get Ami to drive down to collect me once I had the all clear, but still…

Strangely though it felt okay. As we sped through the waves I felt a huge sense of calm. A pair of dolphins jumped from the water and I admired the beautiful sea surrounding us. No panic, no fear, just a peaceful feeling of tranquility knowing everything would be alright.

1 A NEW FOUND PASSION

In my first marriage I had been the stay at home, dependable, play it safe kind of woman. Whenever friends passed my house they would always ring the bell as they knew I would be there. The kettle would spring to life and there would be tea, coffee, milk and a selection of biscuits.

After my divorce I discovered a new sense of purpose and was determined to see more of the world. I had allowed myself to play small, to settle for mediocre as I didn't have the energy for anything else. I had found my wanderlust and life was full of day trips, weekends away and holidays. My awful sense of direction is legendary and this was before GPS, but when you have a willing child with a map on their lap it's amazing how far you can get! Rather than I can't, my attitude became why not!

I met Phil in 2004 and it really was love at first sight. He was fun-loving and up for any adventure, which matched my new found thirst for excitement. Within months we had skiing holidays booked and we'd been indoor climbing, but the hobby with the most impact on our lives by far was scuba diving. When we met, Phil was just about to learn to scuba dive with Clifton Sub Aqua Club or CSAC for short. This was something I had never even thought about doing. I signed up for a try dive just to see what it was like.

A week later I was in a swimming pool, adorned in dive kit floating weightlessly at two metres and my love affair began!

I had never been a technical person only just managing to wire a plug, but soon my belongings included a plethora of wetsuits, drysuits, boots, fins, dive computers, cylinders, regulators…and the list goes on! Some was new, some donated by other members of the diving club we joined but everything went together in a sequence that I quickly learned.

The beauty of the training is the methodical sequence of preparation that you practice again and again and so it becomes second nature. From preparing for a trip and ensuring everything is packed, to getting to the dive site and being ready to go with everything you need on time, practice does indeed make perfect. The training is a mix of theory and practice, of safety and fun.

There is an element of unpredictability that makes diving exciting. The weather is a huge part of this – all the planning in the world can't stop a windy day. There is also a level of fitness needed for diving and a cold can stop play in an instant. Often you can see the sad face of a diver who had been looking forward to their weekend before waking up coughing and full of a cold!

It was after the initial apprehension of something so completely new that I found my inner mermaid – I am a Pisces after all! Once you have ascertained that your kit is put together correctly and working, with everything strapped on correctly you are ready to stride or roll into the sea with a splash! Descending takes a bit of getting used to, remembering to clear your ears and fill your suit with air for comfort, but all the while you are watching the green-blue world around you, watching the fish and waiting for the sea bed or a ship wreck to come into view.

Once at the right depth and comfortable, you can relax into exploring a totally different world. Every dive is different and there is always something new to see. Sea creatures in their own habitat were a delight to behold with shoals of fish, starfish, crabs and the most amazing anemones.

Sunlight dappling through a green-blue haze reveals a beauty that etches into your soul. You may have hours of carrying kit, checking watches and squeezing into uncomfortable suits. You may have bumpy boat journeys and waves of nausea followed by the huffing and puffing of kitting up in a forever moving vessel. You have the initial cold shock of rolling into the water and the inelegant fight to get to the shot line so you can begin your descent.

All this melts into oblivion when you take a moment to survey your surroundings. You are unable to communicate with your fellow divers using words, so expression and body language become paramount. Looking across at your companion to see the look of pure delight is wonderful. You are here on the ocean bed, a place only a fraction of people get to experience. In your secret world you are the explorer, the watcher and the guide. You are sharing a mission to explore wrecks of times gone by, to uncover as many marine species as possible and all the while keeping to time, ensuring safe limits and an event free return to the surface.

Sometimes things go wrong and this is where having a buddy is vital. You can get tangled in a shot line and need a hand to guide you to freedom. You may have a clip undone or your hood caught in your mask and your buddy has much better vision than your mask-restricted view. You may need something more important like air should your equipment fail, so having your buddy close by at all times is not just a luxury! It's great to know that your training has prepared you for most eventualities and you do everything possible to ensure that each dive runs smoothly.

Over time Phil and I developed our own way of diving. Because we dived regularly we got to know each other's routines and could be ready at the same time. Underwater we had the text book signals as well as a few of our own: I'm cold, I'm out of puff or I'm bored would be followed by a plume of bubbles from giggling!

My skills increased as did the depth of my diving! The feeling you get sitting at 50 metres below the sea is exhilarating and peaceful all at once. It's such a feeling to stop for a moment and imagine the volume of water sitting above you.

As members of CSAC we couldn't help but get swept along by the enthusiasm everyone shared. Weekends without the children were spent in various locations around the coast. I had never been camping before, preferring sunny locations and hotels, but rain or shine, off we would go. It must have been quite a shock to my friends and family to see the transformation from cosseted home bird to roaming action woman!

Our outdoor hobbies meant I now possessed thermals, waterproofs and really warm socks as well as skinny jeans and kitten heels. I could be ready at exactly the right time rather than adding five minutes or so. I knew my way around a boat and was catching onto the nautical terms everyone used. Phil got the nickname of "Baz" as someone originally thought his name was Barry, so suddenly I'm calling him Baz while out with friends to some very strange looks!

These days catching us home was a rarity. Ami and Kassi learned to dive too and so our hobby became a family affair. Weekends at the coast now meant a car filled to the gunnels with four sets of dive kit! The girls loved their adventures and I would often smile as they played in the surf in wetsuits. We spent several summers in Tenerife and we all loved being out on the boat in the sunshine and diving in the turquoise water.

It amazed me how a simple hobby had enriched my life so much. I had a host of new skills, a new way to keep fit and a group of amazing, fun-loving friends. From curry nights to weekends away we all came together, not caring what the others did for a living or their histories. What mattered most was where would we be diving next and could we fit in a barbecue.

I got such peace from diving too. I have always had a love of nature but until this point hadn't been able to immerse myself to this level. There was a new level of relaxation I had discovered from being outdoors for days on end. Being out on the ocean felt so peaceful, no mobiles to answer or plans to make…I could just be. Fresh air and exercise gave me an appetite, a sun-kissed glow and of course an even bigger smile.

2 LIVING THE DREAM

There is a phrase I heard when I first ventured out as a self employed person:

"Being an entrepreneur means spending the first three years living the way no one else would, to live the rest of your life the way others only dream of."

I have always been the creative type which means an idea a minute. Quite often an idea strikes in the middle of the night and unless I get up and write it down hours of sleeplessness ensues as my brain runs away with details and new scenarios.

Something else I have discovered over the years – I have a stubborn streak. When I think of something I want to do I will work out how and will go to extreme lengths to make it happen. Even when others suggest giving up I'll go on, seeing it through no matter what.

This has worked really well for me over the years and saw me through eight years of accountancy training, a handful of holistic therapy qualifications and making the huge changes needed to find the right home for my family. I have often wondered what it is that drives me on, something inside that tells me to keep going when I can see the end goal.

Over the years my business has evolved and grown as I have made a succession of ideas happen. With each project I have refined my choices, taking the elements that work and using them again after a few modifications and moving on from the elements that didn't go so well. I have known people who talk about what they will do and never make it happen – this just isn't in my nature. If I think of it, I want to do it. How do you know whether you can if you don't try?

The leap from accountancy to my holistic business was born from my have-a-go nature. The step from the security of employment to self employment was driven by a need for flexibility and freedom. As a single parent working full time I realised there was so much I was missing about my children's lives. Missing sports day or the school play, not being able to help out on school trips and weighing up whether you could take time off when someone was ill gave me huge feelings of guilt. There was also the stress factor of working somewhere you didn't want to be.

I decided that I wanted to work in the evenings when Ami and Kassi were in bed or at weekends when they were with their father. I worked at pamper evenings or went to people's houses, as well as renting a therapy room in various locations.

I then had the notion that I could run my own Mind, Body & Spirit events and made that happen without any prior experience. It's amazing what enthusiasm will make you do - from calling up holistic celebrities and inviting them to speak, to hours of leaflet dropping in the rain! Whenever I realised I had a gap in my skills I would learn how to fill it. From preparing terms and conditions to new ways of marketing. Every step of the way I was working out how to improve and refine my processes.

Again my creative abilities were at play designing catchy names and themes. We had "Sunshine, Strawberries and Psychics" to "The Love Life! Roadshow". From "Spring Into Summer" to "Halloween Happenings"…each one had a great atmosphere and attention to detail.

After several events in a variety of locations I decided it would be better to have a base where people could visit me. As the children were growing up and going to bed later, evenings had become more precious. I wanted to work more through the day and during the week, so found a tiny little base to see if it would work.

For years though I had dreamed of and talked about a project that I held dear: a holistic coffee shop. A place where people could come and enjoy a coffee and a cake and also find out about wellbeing and relaxation. In my mind I saw the front of the shop, complete with a shining and beautiful coffee machine and a display of scrumptious cakes. I saw a rack of personal development books and groups of smiling people chatting happily.

In the back I had pictured relaxing and inviting therapy rooms where the magic really happened. I had learned from firsthand experience how holistic therapies could completely change someone's health and so wanted to let more people know how this worked. I imagined taster days and events where we could educate people on the benefits of different therapies.

I knew from my own experience what it was like to be stressed and unhappy. I wanted my shop to be a place someone could go when they were having a bad day, where they would be welcomed in with a warm smile. My own grandmother seemed to solve everything with a cup of tea and I wanted to continue that tradition.

This idea was big even for me. There was so much I didn't know about running this kind of business. I had no catering experience and had no idea where to start! I knew nothing of hygiene regulations, coffee making or long-term leasing. I would need staff, suppliers, stock and shop fittings.

Over the years I had always talked about 'when I have my coffee shop'. For example, I had decided what coffee brand we would serve, that our cakes would include gluten free choices, that we would have events for authors to launch their books and host courses to teach holistic therapies. Several times I had started to make a plan but it always seemed like a mammoth undertaking and I would shelve the idea for later.

On my 40th birthday I started to plan again. This time I decided to research premises within a 20 minute drive of my house, just to see what properties existed. I had butterflies in my tummy each morning as I searched, was I really going to do this? I told myself to just take one step and see how I felt, this process had always served me well.

Within a few days I had appointments to see three places. The first was over two floors – the coffee shop would be lovely on the ground floor, but the dark basement needed work and would be inaccessible to some of our customers.

The second was tiny! I realised my spacial awareness needed work as I should have worked this out from the estate agent's details. I knew Phil would laugh his head off when I told him, being someone who always knew where North was!

It was on the third viewing that my tummy flipped again. Sitting at the end of a rank of shops was a sad looking empty shop. It looked as if the owners had left in a rush as there were still fittings on the walls. The Estate Agent told me this shop had been empty for two years now and hinted that there could be room for negotiation.

There were three main areas to the premises, lending itself perfectly to a coffee shop and two separate therapy spaces. It would be a big project as we would need to build the kitchen, toilet and partition walls. Again my tummy flipped as I wondered if this was too big an undertaking...but it felt so right.

I put a rather low offer in to the agent and was amazed when it was accepted on the spot. Within just three short weeks I was standing with the keys in my hand, ready for a new chapter.

My Mum & Dad had always been a great support to me at every step in my life, encouraging me and helping in practical ways too. This was no exception – they financed the refit of the shop and even sent some of the guys from their engineering firm to help too. I loved their attitude towards family; nothing was ever too much trouble. It has been such a comfort to know that I can call on my parents at any time, for emotional support, practical advice or just a big hug and a cup of tea.

Those four weeks before our planned opening day had included hours and hours of hard work, training, fact-finding and favours. The whole family pulled together to make it happen. In particular the week before opening had been a challenge, with 6am starts and late night finishes. Phil had lent a hand adding tongue and groove and paint while Ami and Kassi had pitched in with the painting and cleaning, and their barista skills were perfect!

There had been times when I questioned what I was doing: we were all so tired! Our list of things to do had seemed endless. Everything was physically and mentally challenging and so different from anything I had done before. My years of visioning and dreaming carried me through – as well as the excitement of actually opening our doors.

The Witches Brew proudly opened on the 10th April 2010 with a host of friends and family in attendance. We had the shiny coffee machine, lovingly named Fabiana to describe her dark, rich personality and flamboyant heritage. The cakes were exquisite and the atmosphere was warm and welcoming.

Opening night had been a challenge; with thirty guests requiring coffee and cake our barista and waiting skills were put to the test. At one point there were too many cooks in the kitchen and we all had to take a moment and breathe before working out best practices! We had a classic moment when Phil invited the firemen pulled up outside in for a coffee. I have always had a bit of a thing for a fireman – and here were two big burly guys waiting for coffee. I blushed from head to toe and turned into a giggling teenager, to the great amusement of my awesome husband!

My friends and family loved what we had created and it really was a night to remember. We had created a welcoming, relaxing space that would help so many people and I couldn't have been more proud and happy.

I was over the moon that the dream I had created in my imagination was now an exciting reality. Each morning I would raise the shutter, unlock the door and smile as I walked into my shop. We were open six days a week from 9.30am until 4pm with evening events several times a week.

I acknowledged that it wouldn't be easy of course, remembering my entrepreneur promise of hard work followed by living the dream. I had plans for a chain of coffee shops, perhaps a franchised system that would spread the happy word of holistic living and create a community of well and peaceful people.

Ami helped two days a week and Kassi worked at the weekends, and in between I was on my own. We had plenty of customers to talk to and lots to keep me busy, from hygiene and cleaning records to planning our future growth. We had a team of therapists using the back rooms as well as an ever-growing events calendar.

On evenings where we had events I would shut at 4pm and clean up ready to go again at 6pm until late. We had a varied schedule with psychic development classes, business networking, therapist support groups and author launches. We even taught pole dance for ladies confidence and I trained as an instructor – partly to keep fit as well as learning a new skill.

To the outside world I was having a ball and it felt good to have created something so perfect. Initially I was totally happy and relaxed, loving every minute. I would relish showing our visitors around and talking of our plans. We had created so much in such a short space of time I was truly proud of our efforts.

Over time though something changed. Maybe it was tiredness from working so many hours that started my doubt but I began to worry about our success. There was so much to do, could I make it work? Would we attract the customers we needed? Could we turn a profit? Gradually my worries increased and on quiet days I would start to twitch – what if I failed?

My remedy for this was to just work harder. Worry meant I would wake really early, often with something on my mind before I was truly conscious. I would get up and start our marketing and social media posts, getting as much done before jumping in the shower and heading to the shop. In my panic I would skip breakfast, then instead of getting something nourishing I would have a piece of cake and a coffee – perks of the trade I thought.

Once back home the marketing would start again with a newsletter or advertising campaign. I would write lists and plans for future activities and my inner management accountant would come out to play creating budgets and forecasts.

My life to this point showed me that a positive attitude and nourishing mind, body and spirit led to a happy and successful Nicky, but in my panic to have a grown up business I forgot this. It seemed that life had got serious the minute I picked up those keys. That the game stakes had been raised by me stepping out to follow the dream I had wanted for so long. All my holistic knowledge of how to stay well was used for everyone else on a daily basis, but I forgot to use it for me.

I didn't have time to meditate, to exercise or to shop for healthy foods. I was working several nights a week and would arrive home shaking with hunger to ravenously eat the meal Phil had left for me before heading to bed. Sometimes I was so exhausted I would eat it cold, whatever was on the menu.

Our usual evenings of laughter and catching up were infrequent now; if I wasn't at the shop I was poring over a newsletter or drumming up business some other way. When the laptop went away it was because I had nothing left to give and I would head straight to bed myself.

I knew I needed staff but couldn't afford them yet. I knew I needed to outsource my website and marketing but again couldn't work out how to fund that. Every way I could think of making everything easier seemed to be a long way off, requiring us to grow first and I couldn't work out any alternative plan. It seemed my creative brain was silent when it was needed the most.

Gradually the comments started about my appearance as my concerned customers noticed the bags under my eyes. I would wave them away and assure them I was fine, while inwardly wincing that the outside world could see the truth. I'm well known for my colourful clothes and made up public appearance and this would have disguised my fatigue to a point. However I had no time for make up or planning what to wear. As soon as the alarm went off at the ungodly hour I had set for myself, I would stumble into whatever clothes were nearest, eager to make some headway on the road to success.

3 SOME LIGHT RELIEF

With the busy schedule of the coffee shop I hadn't been on one dive trip since opening the shop – that was unheard of. I really had become totally obsessed with working and so in July we decided to go on a long weekend with the diving club. This would be a chance for me to get some diving in and relax a bit – for the first time since opening The Witches Brew. The dive club had a week on Lundy planned and we decided to travel over Friday and dive from Saturday to Wednesday.

Lundy is an island nature reserve in the Bristol Channel. There is a campsite, a pub, a small shop and a few houses and nothing else which sounded perfect to my tired little brain! The club were taking their two RHIBs (Rigid Hull Inflatable Boats) across for an active week of diving the various scenic sites around the Lundy coastline. There would be 24 of us in total, some staying in houses and the rest on the campsite. There would be barbecues, pub meals, fresh air and relaxation.

Ami had been helping me out working part time until this point, but a week before our trip her other job had come to an end. She was unsure what to do next and so I offered her a few weeks' work, to cover me while I went away and to give her some time to plan her future.

Part of me couldn't wait to get diving again and have some relaxation, but another part was terrified of leaving. I wrote lists and reminders galore – even though I knew Ami was completely capable of managing. She had been with me from the beginning, was an accomplished barista with a great work ethic and knew all of our customers. As our trip got closer I could feel my panic rising.

Phil prepared the camping kit and his own kit while I was still busy working. Sensing my stress levels he packed my kit too – something I would normally decline but I had so much to do I could only smile weakly and thank him. I'm sure he would have packed my clothes too if I had asked and I did contemplate it, feeling so short of time.

We were leaving for the ferry at 5am Friday morning and I knew there would be no delaying this. On the Thursday evening we had an event at the shop and I didn't want to cancel, so once the customers had left I washed up and left everything perfectly for Ami to take over. One of my customers – and a lovely friend – stayed to help me tidy up. As we locked up and headed to our cars she gave me a big hug. "Have a lovely time and re-charge your batteries, please?" She said. ""I've been worried about you; you're not looking like yourself."

I promised I would rest and set off for home. As I drove home my mind was racing, trying to check and double check that I had done everything I needed to do. It occurred to me how exhausted I really was, but what could I do? I drove the route on autopilot – I had been doing this journey six days a week every week.

As I got to a really sharp bend a thought popped into my head: what if I just drove straight and didn't take the bend? Everything would stop. There would be peace. This thought had appeared from nowhere, like the voice of a really small, tired and lonely child. For a fleeting moment I considered this thought before my rational mind jumped in. With a shudder I took the corner slowly – and took a steady pace home. Had I really got to the point where I was that tired? Where did that thought come from? I vowed to myself that I would get some rest!

Once at home my panic resumed as I ran around packing my travel bag in the quiet – Phil had already gone to bed ready for our early start. As I went to bed at 12am I set the alarm…for 4am as I had a newsletter to write before I went.

***

Once on Lundy I began to relax. We put up the tent and made our home from home. This really was a deserted island, our surroundings were beautiful and there seemed to be so much empty space – a perfect spot for a relaxed CSAC trip and I was looking forward to the weekend ahead. We stored our dive kit on the quay ready for the early start in the morning and waved goodbye to the ferry that wouldn't return until the following Tuesday.

Phone signal was sparse here too, which was cause for a bit of concern, but I was sure that Ami would be able to reach one of our phones if she needed to. Perhaps I really could relax a bit and rest my poor frazzled brain. Walking back up to the campsite was a bit of a heave – it was nicknamed Cardiac Hill and I could see why! After the initial concrete path the slope got steeper with uneven grassy bits and then some steps before grass again. It seemed to go on forever and as I panted and puffed I promised myself that I would get fit again.

The last few months had been an amazing journey, but I had paid a large price in time, energy and mental capacity. I resolved that once I got home I would sit down with Ami and brainstorm to make a plan for the coming months. There was so much I loved about running the coffee shop, our customers were lovely and we were creating the community spirit that was so important to us. We had created a strong brand with a real passion behind it and I could really see how this could grow into a chain or franchise.

The downside was six days a week in the same place and the ever increasing 'to do' list. To be innovative required always doing new activities, creating new services or working in new ways. However much we accomplished there always seemed so much more to do. We were turning over cash but there was so much more to invest in to complete the picture and our overheads were really high. Still, I would leave all that aside for now and enjoy my holiday!

Our evening was spent as a group in the warm and welcoming pub. A glass of red wine helped the relaxation even further and we headed to bed around 9pm, excitedly talking about tomorrow's diving. We tucked up in the tent, cuddling up to giggle and chat like we always did before my evening working made this a rarity.

The next morning we were all up early, excited and ready to get diving. It had rained a little the day before, but today we had blue skies and calm seas much to our delight. The divers were a self sufficient bunch and had all brought camping stoves and plenty of coffee. We had bought bacon from the tiny little shop the day before and so soon there was a sizzle in the air! We all had to laugh when a canny seagull seized it's chance for a steal when Berenice turned away to get the ketchup – as quick as a flash the dastardly gull swooped in and grabbed all four slices of bacon from the pan.

Berenice's look of complete puzzlement added perfectly to the picture while she worked out what had happened to breakfast. We all looked on roaring with laughter…and donated a rasher each to go with her roll and ketchup!

Down on the quay there was hustle and bustle as 24 of us tried to get into some sort of order. There was a diving schedule, a list of people and time slots for everyone. A Coxswain had been allocated for each dive and Phil took the early turn, leaving me to get my kit together ready to join him for the second wave.

I checked through all of my kit, which had been packed beautifully with everything I needed. I smiled at my luck of having such a thoughtful and competent husband then set about assembling, checking and packing everything so that when the boat came in I would be ready. I had always been late for everything in my youth, but diving had changed all that!

The boat returned with an excited group of divers all talking about the first dive. There had been sightings of wrasse (a club joke that all fish were indeed wrasse) and allegedly mermaids and dolphins too. It's not just fishermen that reserved the right to exaggerate it seemed. Our motto was to never let the truth get in the way of a good story and this time was no exception.

The one thing you quickly learn about diving is that you can never have too much kit. It took a while for everyone to unload the various mesh bags, scuba gear, cameras, torches, spares and food parcels, with everyone making a human chain to make the experience as quick as possible. Then we all reversed the action to re-load the boat with our equipment.

Once on board I checked to make sure everything I needed was here as a diver on the previous wave had got out to the dive location to realise his mesh bag containing fins, mask and computers was still on the quay. Each year we have an award to be won called the 'Left Behind Award' and it wasn't going to be me that got it!

The journey out to the various dive sites the club visited was something I enjoyed once I got the hang of holding on and reading the bounce of the waves. RHIBs are great little boats, versatile and fun to drive but an unexpected wave can easily take you out of your seat. I had recently qualified as a boat handler and I loved being out on the sea with the wind in my hair. This was something else I had never thought I would do, another string to my 'action girl' bow.

Soon we were on the site and the kitting up commenced. There isn't much room on a boat full of divers with six people to get ready and in the water. Depending on which sites you choose there is often a window of diving time due to the tides and so efficiency can be critical. Each buddy pair kits up in turn with everyone else lending a hand. The great thing I had found about divers is that when you are all very literally in the same boat everyone helps everyone else.

Phil and I kitted up and it was a bit of a struggle to reach my fins now that my tummy had expanded of late. Again I wished that there was a gym next door to The Witches Brew as that really was the only way I would get fit at this rate, unless we altered our menu to only serve salad!

Somehow I managed to get everything on and we went through our safety brief. No matter how many times we had dived together this was still part of our routine as it's so easy to forget something. Soon we were ready and with a "1, 2, 3… Go!" from our skipper we rolled backwards into the cold and instantly invigorating water.

Investing in a dry suit meant that only my head and hands were in the cold water, but it can still be a bit of an initial shock when you roll in. Elegance and diving definitely do not go together! I gathered myself the right way up, headed to the shot line and our diving adventure began.

Descending into the green depths I cleared the pressure in my ears and checked my depth, feeling a little rusty as I hadn't dived much so far that year. My breathing rate was a little higher than normal and I consciously began to slow it down to ensure we got a good dive time. It's amazing how being stressed can mean you use up your air at a much faster rate and curtail the planned dive.

Once at 24 metres we had a kit check and then started off to explore. Before diving in the sea I had no idea of the beauty I would discover down at these depths. There is striking topography to behold with pinnacles and crevices galore, kelp and seaweed and a variety of urchins and anemones.

I wasn't great at remembering the names of what I saw, but appreciated the beauty nonetheless. There were plenty of fish in residence as well as starfish and crabs, on some dives you could collect scallops and even the odd lobster – if you were brave enough! Some divers are hunter gatherers loving the thrill of the chase, others live to explore wrecks and turn their noses up at 'fluffy' dives which involve pure scenery.

I liked a mixture of both – happy with whatever I found as long as there were critters to play with. I was happy to lead or be led and would point out what I saw to Phil along the way. If there was a shot line to get back to I usually let Phil lead the way as my sense of direction under water is no better than on land!

The aim of a good diver is to be close enough to the bottom to see everything, but to practise good buoyancy so you don't trash the homes of all the local residents. I had done my share of bouncing along the bottom initially, but through controlled breathing and practise could usually keep a good depth without too much effort!

I had been so preoccupied with our descent and initial route that it was only after 15 minutes I realised my drysuit valve was still open – I wondered why everything felt such a squeeze! I closed the valve and added some air, instantly adding to my comfort and warmth. There was a bit of current that we were swimming against and so the exercise had meant I hadn't got too cold by the time I noticed.

After about half an hour though the chill set in and I felt uncomfortable. With the current against us we had finned quite hard, so I signalled to Phil that I wanted to head back to the surface. It takes a while to ascend as you have a decompression stop at six metres for three minutes or more depending on your depth and dive time. Those three minutes seemed to go on forever, I craved a nice cup of tea!

Once on the surface I handed my weight belt and kit to my fellow divers waiting on the boat and heaved myself in. Some folk manage an elegant entry with a few bounces and a kick of their fins to land on the tubes looking relaxed. I too bounce and kick but only ever manage to get half in before I need to be grabbed by the elbows and manhandled into the hull. I then lie like a beached whale until someone takes pity on me and removes my fins. I have come to accept that this is how it is for me!

We were soon back at the quay and after repeating the unload/reload sequence the next group headed off for their adventures. We wandered over to the tiny shack where the kettle lived with a steaming mug of coffee. We had a while to go before our second dive so plenty of time for lunch, a wander and a sun bathe.

The boat took longer than planned to return for our afternoon dive and it was about 4pm when we spotted the RHIB coming around the corner. We were all waiting with our kit on the jetty ready for the swift changeover. It was here when I saw the boat come into view that I heard a little voice from within say, "I don't want to dive." A feeling of hesitance settled in my tummy, which was unusual as we always did two dives a day on any trips.

I thought about how busy I had been lately and felt sleepy laying in the sunshine. I decided not to be a lazy bones, after all I wouldn't get as many chances to dive this year with running a busy coffee shop. I hauled myself to my feet, had a good stretch and set about loading my kit onto the boat.

This time our descent was more fraught than usual as my mask, which I had worn on lots of dives, developed a slow leak. Try as I might I couldn't get it to stop despite some assistance from Phil. Once at 15 metres and on the sea bed I cleared the sea water that was making my eyes sting and we started to swim. Still the mask leaked at a slow rate and so periodically I had to stop and empty the water. My eyes were sore and I was grumpy. I couldn't find any reason for this, my hood didn't seem to be tucked into it and the mask felt tight enough, so I silently grumbled some more and carried on.

To add to my discomfort the current had increased since lunch and we were swimming against it. A few times I had to tap Phil to stop while I caught my breath. I couldn't seem to get comfortable in the water and had trouble holding a steady depth. One minute I was inflating my wing to lift myself from the bottom and the next I was dumping air as I was starting to ascend.

I growled to myself – being the only way I could express my frustrations. Phil could see I was having a few challenges and checked to see if I was okay with a signal. I signalled yes, I was okay, despite my inner mutterings of how I should get a grip of myself, get my kit in order and get back to diving properly!

After another thirty minute dive my eyes were sore, I was tired from the effort of swimming against the current and again quite cold. I gave Phil the thumbs up which meant "Can we go now please?" and we started our ascent. Once back on the boat and able to talk I recounted my dive to Phil – not that I needed to really as my bloodshot eyes and blue lips told most of the story!

Back at the quay I was able to warm up in the sunshine, again with a nice cuppa and we packed everything away ready to do it all again the next day. Even when a dive doesn't go to plan, the passion creeps back in and you are soon planning your next outing.

4 CARDIAC HILL AND BEYOND

Later that afternoon our group decided to head back up to the campsite, the thought of a hot shower and a snooze before our evening meal at the pub was an enticing one. Once again we commented on how there should be a jeep running up and down Cardiac Hill.

Phil and I were holding hands, chatting and giggling for a while…but this had to stop as the incline increased. The further up we got the harder it got to breathe and about half way up I couldn't even speak, tapping Phil's arm to stop.

He looked concerned but I could only smile weakly, I had absolutely no breath left. My chest was tight and every breath was a struggle. I tried bending double and standing up straight, nothing seemed to help and I started to panic. After a couple of minutes of stillness gradually my breathing returned to normal. For probably the hundredth time that weekend I promised and vowed I would take more care and get fit. We took a much slower pace this time and finished our climb to the campsite.

I didn't say much about that to the rest of the group, choosing to make light of it, but I was really rattled. How could I have lost my breath that badly that I couldn't even speak? I knew the last few months had been a challenge but I knew that now was the time to make some changes. When we got home I needed to make a plan.

The pub did us proud that evening with great food and I enjoyed a glass of wine to wash it down too. Most of the group joined us and so there was plenty of laughter and tales of previous trips, with exaggerations and embellishments thrown in as usual. The good thing about our number was that we could have an instantly great atmosphere and make our own fun. We had differing ages, vocations and circumstances but our shared passion made for easy conversation.

Fresh air and diving is a wonderful combination, but by 10pm most of us were ready for bed and we had a 7am start in the morning. With full bellies we wandered back to the campsite and tucked up for the night.

I must have been in a really deep sleep that night, as it took me a while to wake up enough to realise that I couldn't breathe properly. If I laid flat on my back I could breathe to a point, but any attempt to turn on my side had me gasping for breath. I looked at my watch, it was 5am and Phil was clearly not disturbed by my fidgeting as I could hear his deep breathing, steady and even.

I decided to go for a walk to see if I felt better, which was quite a struggle as the slightest movement made me lose my breath. I had pain high up in my chest so I knew something was wrong. I thought perhaps I had pulled my chest muscles getting into the boat the previous day.

I didn't want to disturb anyone this early, so slowly walked around the field in the early light, experimenting with movement and stretches. Any form of bending made breathing impossible, but with an upright stance and a slow pace there was just the pain to contend with. I was feeling the panic begin to rise – could this level of pain really be a pulled muscle? I realised that my diving would be off today whatever it was and that made me sad.

By 6.30am when Phil poked his head from the tent to see where I was I had tears rolling down my face, hurting and afraid. I am quite a baby and complain about bruises and any form of bump, but from his face I could see that he was concerned. He tried to hide it with a smile and a hug but I knew him well enough by now.

Lightly he suggested packing a bag with my wash kit in and some spare clothes 'just in case' and heading off to see Helen, who was our dive club medic and was also on the trip staying at the house half way down the hill.

His tone may have been light but for someone who has had no need to see a doctor in five years or more I knew he was taking this seriously. Slowly we made our way down what seemed a never-ending hill due to my slow pace and frequent stops to catch what little breath I had. Although not at the house, we found Helen on the quay.

News of my predicament soon spread through our group and I knew I was in the hands of caring people. It all felt very strained and I didn't feel comfortable with all the attention, so suggested Phil head off for his first dive. There was no ferry that day so where was I going to go I joked, trying to use my default defence of humour. This backfired totally as the laughter took my breath away and I had to sit on a rock to recover.

I was obviously convincing enough though as off he went with the first group. I wandered around the corner and in private allowed the tears to flow once more. This wasn't part of the plan. I had come away for a rest and to do something I loved, not to get hurt. I felt really fragile and really old, I assumed due to the lack of oxygen I was getting but it still wasn't a nice feeling. I wanted to magically start to feel better so that everything could go back to normal. I was too busy with the shop to take a few days' rest, so this needed to go away now. A fresh batch of tears started to fall just as the cavalry arrived with a cup of tea and a cuddle.

Helen re-appeared after ringing the Diver Diseases Research Centre in Plymouth. They are the first point of call for any diver related injury or accident and their knowledge and expertise is second to none we were told in our training.

They suggested a chest X-Ray at Barnstaple hospital. With the absence of a ferry I jokingly suggested we call a helicopter, but my smile froze when Helen said she suspected a pneumothorax (punctured lung) so I couldn't be at altitude. I pushed away the little voice that taunted me, saying it couldn't just be a pulled muscle. Any other suggestion had bigger consequences that I didn't want to event think of.

The next suggestion was that one of the RHIBs could take me across the channel. I was hesitant to do this as the slightest movement meant I lost my breath, so a bouncing boat could make for a very uncomfortable crossing. On cue the boats came back from the first dive and Phil joined our small group, agreeing that the RHIB may be the only option, if far from a perfect choice. I knew my options were limited, but I just wanted someone to wave a magic wand and make me better again, please?

Looking around trying to brush off the seriousness of this conversation I could see another RHIB coming into view. This one was much bigger, with three men in yellow waterproofs coming our way. The Devon Coastguard were out on patrol and had decided to come and say hello. Helen went off to the quay to meet them as it seemed another solution had presented itself.

It turned out the coastguards had been sailing around Lundy as the island is a zone where fishing is prohibited. They'd spotted our group and decided to stop; usually they just drive around the island and head back to the mainland. After Helen explained my predicament they had offered to take me across to Ilfracombe and the Harbour Master would call me an ambulance. DDRC had been clear in their advice – no taxi or other transport, only an ambulance would do.

I couldn't believe that I was causing so much fuss – ambulances were for really sick people surely? Helen must have seen my reticence and did a great job of keeping me calm while efficiently ensuring we got under way quickly. I was lent a better waterproof coat and bag as the 23 mile journey back to the mainland would be quite different on a RHIB to the ferry!

As we pulled away from the jetty I waved to my Phil, the man I should have asked to come with me but who was now getting further and further away from my side. I turned out to sea to hide my tears from the three strapping coastguards who got called out to emergencies on a regular basis. They were capable, professionally trained and used to adversity. I, however felt lost, afraid and completely out of my depth.

In recent years I had taken charge of my own wellbeing learning Reiki, meditation and positive thinking to keep me well and following my intuition over every decision. I never caught colds or flu or needed to visit the doctor. So why then was I currently heading to hospital? What had led me to a point where I was clearly broken? I had changed my life for the better in so many ways and had never been afraid of taking a new direction, so why did I feel completely stuck?

As I studied the ocean intently a pod of three dolphins jumped and glided by our side, just long enough to be noticed before diving back down out of view. It was a sunny, calm and beautiful day and I took in my wonderful surroundings as a silver lining to my current cloud.

I took a deep breath, painted a smile on my face and turned back to my fellow travellers. They were each taking turns to check on me, talking in hushed voices and I couldn't help noticing how fast we were going. I hoped it was just their tea time that meant we were expertly weaving along the crest of the waves at such a pace.

Soon enough the coastline came into view; we were nearly at our destination. I was holding onto the seat in front of me with both hands, when suddenly my left arm dropped to my side. I raised my arm and held on again, but once more my grip slipped and my arm dropped to my side. Then the fizzing started.

During dive training, Decompression Injury (DCI) or 'The Bends' is covered extensively. Here is the theory:

As we descend the pressure on our body builds. At ten metres the pressure doubles and then increases proportionately the deeper you go. At 20 metres you have three times the pressure on you than you would on the surface.

The air we breathe is 78% nitrogen, along with 21% oxygen and small amounts of other gases. During a dive the body takes on nitrogen, which gets stored in the soft tissues. When you take on nitrogen at depth the bubbles are small. As you ascend at a controlled pace the bubbles gradually increase to normal size and most of the bubbles leave the body, with the rest naturally going over time.

If you suddenly ascend after a dive, either by coming up too quickly or getting on a flight then the bubbles go from small to large at a quick pace. These bubbles then get stuck in the soft tissues, causing pain and a fizzing sensation as they try to leave the body but get stuck by the joints, hence the name of the bends as it's usually an elbow or knee that gets the pain. Imagine the pressure inside of a bottle of champagne; this gives you an idea of what can happen in the body. Because of this you are not allowed to fly for a period after a dive and why we have a surface interval between dives, giving the body time to recover.

My whole arm felt like it was filled with fizzy lemonade and pain had started to build in my shoulder. My blood ran cold at the realisation: I had a bend. The whole morning I had been talking myself out of any scenario that seemed scary; I had just pulled a muscle. The hospital would check me over, but I would get a clean bill of health and be sent on my way. I would call Ami to pop down to Barnstaple and I would be home before bedtime.

Now however, pulling into Ilfracombe harbour on this lovely sunny day I knew that I had a bend. I would go to Barnstaple, but then I expected to be sent on to the Diver Diseases Centre in Plymouth. No early bed and a story for the annual dive club dinner, this was serious. I wanted Phil but there was no ferry from Lundy until Wednesday, his only option had been coming with me and I had refused. I was in pain, I could hardly breathe, I had a fizzing arm and no idea what would happen next.

5 THE CAVALRY RALLIES

As we pulled into the harbour steps my body seemed to belong to someone else… it didn't seem to be accepting orders from me anyway. The coastguards were busy mooring up the boat as quickly as possible, intent on getting me the medical help I needed and as yet unaware of the recent developments. I felt weak and disorientated and gratefully accepted the steadying hand and offer to carry my bag. As a diver you are always responsible for carrying your own stuff, the phrase being, "If you can't carry it you shouldn't be diving with it!" but here I was handing everything over without so much as a no thank you.

My muscles appeared to have been replaced with wobbling jelly as I stepped onto the quayside and grabbed on to the handrail. The slight exercise had taken most of my breath, but now I was aware that my vision was changing… the world appeared to be taking on a yellowish tinge, as if I was looking at an old sepia coloured photograph. Everything seemed to be happening in slow motion and I felt older than ever.

Gradually I made my way up what seemed like a thousand steps and allowed myself to be led to the Harbour Master's office. My rescuers explained my plight and passed on the recommendation of an ambulance. I was instantly met with warm smiles and reassuring words and while dialling 999 the Harbour Master asked a few questions. To start with: what was my name?

In my time I have enjoyed three surnames but had lived with my first name quite happily for forty years, so why now could I not remember it? I was searching the memory banks which usually took less than a second, only now there was just a foggy silence. What was going on? I could see everyone looking at me expectantly, but for what seemed like an eternity nothing was happening for me. Eventually the magic cog turned over and I remembered, phew!

This sequence happened for every question: where had we been diving? How many dives? What depths? Had I come up too fast? Did I need anything? Each question led to the same response, seconds ticking past loudly with no answers coming forward. It was like being used to a Ferrari and it being replaced by a Morris Minor; what I had relied upon for lightning speed and an accurate answer, followed by a witty comment and a flashy smile was now as slow as a sleepy snail and all I could do was smile weakly and do my best.

I was too tired to panic and too confused to think about what all this meant. Processing anything seemed beyond my capability, so I just stuck with the knowledge that something was seriously wrong with me and perhaps that ambulance was a good idea after all.

Luckily there were no sirens, but there were blue flashing lights and two more smiling faces. The handover was efficiently and caringly handled, with all the information gained so far passed across along with the instructions from Helen and the DDRC.

Everyone wished me well and I thanked them and smiled. It didn't seem enough at that point, how can you thank someone enough when you are in the midst of mental chaos? I didn't feel I was doing justice to this group of people who had taken such care for my wellbeing, but the enormity of my situation was nowhere near sinking in properly.

Once in the ambulance I was given a thorough check over and mentioned my fizzing, floppy arm. Soon we were on our way to Barnstaple hospital and my crew chatted happily about the weather, last night's television and any other subject to distract me which I welcomed. Again I felt a wave of calm wash over me; it was all going to be okay.

Initially when I arrived in Barnstaple hospital the fact that I was a diver was received with much scratching of heads. The wonderful doctor that went on to assess me explained that I wasn't her area of expertise, but that she would do some initial examinations and then get on the phone to the DDRC. My blood pressure was fine, my breathing was poor and when we got onto the muscle testing all my poorly left arm could do was buckle from the slightest push rather than resist as it had always done.

It was if there were two of me looking on here. The first was fascinated by my physical frailties, marvelling at how one arm could be fine and the other a total sponge. The second was screaming to get a panic on, to shout and make a fuss so that we could make this go away quicker. Part of me was peaceful, part of me terrified.

After a quick call to DDRC I was given an oxygen mask, being the first step of treatment while they organised a chest X Ray for me. I was then, due to the obvious weakness in my arm, going to be dispatched down to the DDRC in Plymouth for more tests and expert care.

I had asked Phil to call my daughter Ami as I left Lundy, thinking that she would be the least likely to panic and therefore able to calmly tell my parents. As I looked at my signal-less phone I wondered what to do next, as I wouldn't be in Barnstaple for much longer as I had originally thought. I didn't need to worry for long, a nurse could tell me that my family had rung and they had been told I would be off to Plymouth soon enough. I hoped I would get some phone signal on the way.

The chest X Ray came back clear – a punctured lung was thankfully ruled out, so even though my breathing was still laboured I wouldn't need a biro inserted into my chest like they did on Casualty!

In forty years I had completely avoided ambulances or any kind of medical emergency apart from a slight break in my arm at 10. Yet here I was in my second ambulance of the day, on a stretcher with my own supply of oxygen destined for Plymouth. On the one hand it was all quite exciting and the oxygen had certainly improved my clarity while reducing the pain in my shoulder. Yet on the other I would have in a flash given anything to be in my warm sleeping bag on Lundy cuddled up with my hubby.

In between oxygen inhaling and chatting to the marvellous guy checking up on me I got enough signal to ring Phil. As I told him of my progress so far and obvious bend it broke my heart to hear the worry in his voice.

No matter how many times I told him I was fine, I was being looked after and that there was nothing he could do I could tell he wanted to be at my side. Of course being practical I knew this wasn't possible and we soon moved on to jokes about the wild parties he could have on Lundy without me and how if he spotted any John Dory's or mermaids then he would owe me several beers. I agreed to keep him posted and quickly hung up before the giggles turned to tears.

Next I rang Ami. She had been with Mum and Dad when Phil called so had no time to play it down or put on a poker face before letting them know where I was. Ami had this practical, clear thinking ability and often took the grown up stance in our relationship. I joked a lot that she was in fact my parent not the other way around. I was so proud to hear how she had organised everyone, calmly hatched several plans depending on when I needed fetching and still managed to joke about never letting me out of her sight again. Again I managed a call without tears. I wondered if it was shock, as usually I would have been in floods. Perhaps my brain was busy trying to make sense of everything.

After making my calls I went back to my oxygen, too tired for any more conversations with my ambulance man. In moments I could feel myself slipping into that pre-sleep state, where your whole body is heavy and the world seems to be slipping away. That one day already felt like a lifetime and I let myself drift off to sleep.

***

By the time we arrived at the Diver Diseases Research Centre in Plymouth it was 11pm at night, so it felt as if we were sneaking into some secret laboratory...which in effect we were!

The duty doctor had been called out, a young, studious man intent on being as thorough as possible. He carried out his tests and asked his questions, studied my dive computer and gave little away. It seemed that the oxygen had cleared away my brain fog and I was able to answer his questions efficiently. My usual attempts at sarcasm and humour went completely unnoticed; here was a man on a mission.

The physical tests were highlighting several facts: the oxygen had improved the weakness in my arm and the pain in my shoulder to some extent already, a sign that it was a Decompression Injury. My vital signs were all normal so there didn't seem to be anything else going on. I had suffered a muscular (lungs and arm), skeletal (shoulder) and cerebral (brain) bend.

Wow. To hear the final diagnosis put in this way made it sound serious indeed and I was glad the peaceful serenity that had served me so well up to this point stayed as my main emotion. There were no tears, no jokes and no questions, it seemed simple acceptance was my method of choice tonight.

The treatments for decompression illness and injury had been tested over many years, with initial diving limits being calculated by studying the effects of nitrogen on large numbers of Navy divers. It cannot be an exact science as everyone has slightly differing physiology: one person will act in a different way to another who does exactly the same activity.

The first course of action is always to administer oxygen and then to re-compress, i.e. to take the body back to the same pressure as if still at depth. This compresses the nitrogen bubbles back to a small size and then by gradually decreasing the pressure over a long period of time you give the body a better chance to release a lot more nitrogen naturally as you breathe. Back to the champagne analogy – releasing the cork very, very slowly!

My treatment was to 'dive' down to a simulated depth of 60 metres and to be given 100% oxygen. I would then be brought 'back up' to normal pressure. The procedure would take six hours and the hope was that my symptoms would disappear. Of course there were no promises, but that was the plan.

The decompression chamber had been used originally by deep sea divers years ago and it felt quite surreal to walk in and have the door sealed behind me. I was accompanied on my 'dive' by a wonderful nurse, who would check my vital signs and keep an eye on me. She would experience the same pressure as me.

I had been given some hospital issue pyjamas but was unprepared for the plastic helmet complete with rubber neck seal…this was never covered in

BSAC or PADI training! This was how they would administer 100% oxygen for prolonged periods during my six hour journey. It seemed that the night could only get more surreal…

There was no time to stop and think about what was going on here. Usually when I needed any kind of procedure I would make an appointment, go away and think about it and then be ready on the day. Here I had to be ready now, to dive right in – literally!

I began to wonder whether the calm, peaceful approach was just delayed shock, or was I really that poorly that I had no fight left? The weeks and months of high stress and organisation seemed a world away from this version of me – quietly going along with my instructions smiling weakly.

Once we were locked in and comfortable the pressurising began and we needed to equalise the pressure in our ears as if on any normal dive. This was quite intense: in a normal dive you can go back up but here we were in a computer operated chamber. I had been warned what could go wrong with my hearing if I couldn't equalise, so this was the important bit for me. My brain started to play tricks – were my ears okay? Really? They were and I was relieved when we were at our destined pressure and I could stop pinching my nose and blowing as well as wriggling my ears, moving my jaw and swallowing - using all the techniques I had learned over years of dives in unison.

The following 6 hours were spent wearing my very fetching plastic hood for long periods of time, with gaps of respite in between. There was a choice of movies and we chose something with Cameron Diaz, although exactly what I can't recall. The adventures of the day had exhausted me completely and I slept, using my hair as a cushion against the plastic. When I awoke the nurse congratulated me on my efforts as she had never seen anyone sleep with the helmet on. It appeared my Mum's description that I could sleep on a washing line could, in fact, be true!

After our 'ascent' back to normal pressure tests showed that my symptoms and weakness had improved. I was sent in ambulance number three to Derryford hospital for some overnight bed rest. The whole day seemed very surreal in the moments when I thought about my current surroundings. On the whole though tiredness won out and I napped fairly well, oblivious to the usual comings and goings of a busy ward in a hospital.

The next morning I was collected bright and early and escorted back to the DDRC for my appointment with Phil Bryson. Speaking to people since, Phil's knowledge is legendary on diver diseases and its treatment. My initial experience was of a caring, enlightening and thorough doctor who was intent on giving me all the facts I needed, as well as reassurance and advice.

Tests showed I had responded well to my treatment, my arm was resisting nicely and the pain in my shoulder had gone. I was alert and well and therefore free to go. I was dispatched into the waiting room to watch daytime television while Ami and Dad winged their way to Plymouth.

As I sat there, with my dive bag and waterproof jacket for company I felt like I was watching someone else's life. People were coming and going as the chambers are used to treat other conditions like cancer and wound healing. These people were scheduled in and expected, they all knew each other due to their regular visits and knew the routine.

I felt like I had been dropped in from Mars, shell shock and disorientation stunning me into silence. When working in the shop I had a smile for everyone; I would start a conversation at the drop of a hat and made everyone at ease. Here I had no clue what to do and no energy to do it. I watched the television without actually watching; something I had learned to do in my unhappy first marriage – appear normal to the world around while everything inside is churning.

I was too tired to do anything but sit, but I felt twitchy and on edge. I wanted to walk around, call a friend, do some work, run away…but could only sit and watch the hours, knowing that my rescuers were doing everything they could to get to me.

It was such a relief to see friendly faces when the cavalry arrived several hours later and I resisted the strong urge to collapse into floods of tears as Ami gave me a hug. She and Dad helped out by telling their tales of Mum's panic and Dad's navigation which was a wonderful distraction.

As I ventured out into the daylight I was immediately struck by how short sighted I was. I usually wore glasses for driving and one of the temporary side effects of recompression is short sight, but I could hardly read anything. Rather than fear I was starting to find the whole thing fascinating. I remember a phrase on a fridge magnet once that read, "People plan while God laughs." I really did feel as if I was being swept along and had no option but to simply go with the flow and accept life as it unfolded.

6 BACK TO NORMAL

Arriving at home was a strange experience, as if a lifetime had passed rather than a few days. Ami made a coffee while Dad chatted away and I greeted a rather disgruntled Izzy the cat who always sulked when we left her. In a way it was nice to get this normal response as everything else seemed so weird!

Ami would be looking after the shop for the next week at least and she did not want to see me in there. Apparently running The Witches Brew had been easy business and she couldn't see why I worked so many hours, she said. I decided not to go into the details of endless marketing, planning and accounts, being really thankful for one less thing to worry about for the time being.

I really did appreciate having such a close knit and wonderful family, they had taken care of everything including food supplies. As Kassi was out for the evening I would be fine on my own. As Dad said goodbye and went back to the car Ami lagged behind. Seriously she looked at me with her gorgeous brown eyes. "Mum, you will take care won't you; you do know you could have died?"

"Don't be silly Love." I said, trying to detract from the suddenly grave turn of our conversation. "Really Mum, I just want you to know how serious this is, people do die of bends as you well know." I gave her another huge hug, "I'm not going anywhere Sweetheart, I have too much to do to be leaving quite so soon." I knew there would be a full version of this conversation in the future, but for now my wise soul of a daughter left it at that and followed her Granddad to the car.

Phil wouldn't be home until the following evening, so I set about resting some more and watching mindless television - again. I had been warned that recompression was tiring and I suppose a coastguard rescue mission, my ambulance rides and late night escapades had taken their toll too. By 8pm I was fast, fast asleep.

I woke up around 9am with nothing to do but rest. The house was quiet and I wandered about, not quite sure how to be still. Since February life had been one speed – break-neck. There had always been such a big list of things to do it was always a case of prioritising. I hadn't had time to read, to listen to music or to watch the TV unless I was working on the laptop at the same time.

Ah, the laptop – I could at least check some e-mails. While it fired up I made a fresh cup of coffee, intent on doing something that resembled normal. Within a minute of typing I had to stop, the fizzing from the previous day started again as if a swarm of bees had taken residence in my arm. My heart sank – had I really thought it would all be that easy? I had assumed my bend had been a warning to slow down and my recovery had been instant. It seemed I would be going with the flow a while longer as this version of events was not in my hands.

I rang the DDRC and spoke again to Phil Bryson. Apparently this could happen in certain cases and was nothing to worry about. As I focused on my body to mentally assess how I was feeling I noticed a new sensation too: although I was standing with my full weight on my left leg somehow I couldn't really feel it…

It was decided that as Phil was due home that evening my treatment could wait until the following day. We would be expected at DDRC by 9am the next morning when I would once again enjoy a 'dive'.

Soon the house was bustling as my concerned Mum came to my aid. My hug was sharply interrupted by her remembering she had left something in her bag - well known code used in our family for hiding tears and outbursts of emotion. I was pleased we could distract ourselves and change the subject, as I wasn't quite sure what was going on and a good cry would just be too exhausting right now. So we set about general tidying and idle chatter as well as packing a bag for tomorrow's journey.

Phil arrived around 8pm and I was so pleased to be wrapped in his arms. What is it about a big hug that makes everything feel instantly okay? He had been worried sick, could hardly get any phone signal and had been cursing himself for not coming with me. Bless my husband for being perfect!

I had a curry ready for my ravenous traveller. I was not known for my culinary skills, usually burning everything in sight but had learned a regulation curry for just such occasions and had worked hard not to ruin it. As we sat with our curry and a glass of red wine - standard chilling aids - I lightly asked, "Do you fancy a trip to Plymouth tomorrow?"

7 ON THE ROAD AGAIN

I introduced Phil Marshall to Phil Bryson and the two men shook hands. After my current weaknesses were assessed another six hour recompression was planned. During this time Phil would enjoy a tour of the facilities, something which I could tell he was looking forward to being an engineer at heart. As divers we have always taken safety very seriously and had learned all the theory behind the body and the effects of nitrogen, as well as rescue skills and diver first aid. Here was the opportunity for a very practical lesson and one I knew Phil would love.

He had always loved the technical side of diving, upgrading his kit from single cylinder diving to a twin set and learning new gas mixing for diving at a deeper range. He dreamed of a Rebreather, a way of diving to deeper depths for longer periods. Where I was happy to plateau and enjoy depths of 50 metres and no more he had already qualified to 60 metres and had deeper dives planned for the future.

After another six hour trip complete with plastic hat and very fetching pyjamas, again my symptoms disappeared including the weakness in my leg. This was encouraging of course, but due to my relapse the previous day it was decided that I should have a shorter burst of recompression the next morning for good measure. We were sent to the neighbouring respite centre that was used by DDRC and the Heart Foundation for patients and carers.

As we left Phil Bryson waved us off and gave his care instructions to my husband. I could be taken on a date to a local curry house and enjoy a single glass of red wine, but I was to be in bed by 9pm and returned to the centre the next morning. For a usually strong, independent and capable woman I felt a huge amount of relief at hearing that just for once I could relax and let go of any responsibility.

Our evening out was an enjoyable one, Phil played host with a mischievous smile and a flourish of door opening and attentiveness. For the last few months we really had been like ships passing in the night and even our welcomed break away had mostly been spent apart due to my body's shenanigans.

In our six years together we had never had one argument, any disagreements had been calmly talked through which always surprised our friends. We spent our days together working as a team giggling and enjoying our own world. We enjoyed holidays and fun with our friends, but were equally as happy at home doing nothing. I truly had met my soul mate.

We knew that my bend would mean a certain amount of time with no diving and we had holidays planned in the Isles of Scilly and Tenerife later that year. For now we decided to play it all by ear, to see what happened next and to rely on the advice of the DDRC and of course Helen our club medic.

My recompression trip the following day was only two hours long and so by lunchtime we were able to head home. I was well rested and relaxed and my symptoms were gone. A letter would be sent to my GP and further tests were needed.

According to Phil Bryson a cause isn't found for 40% of diver bends, sometimes it can be a fast ascent or other medical reason but for some a reason is never found. In my case though they couldn't work out how the nitrogen had got into my lungs and brain. I would need a test for a hole in the heart and lung function to rule out any underlying conditions.

Of course I didn't relish this news; I stayed away from my GP as much as possible preferring to find natural remedies where I could. It wasn't that I shunned orthodox treatment; I had huge admiration for medical advances and acknowledged that there was a time and valuable place for drugs and surgery. I just liked to try simpler methods first.

I was hoping after my recompression that I would be able to get back to some semblance of normality and my brand new business that needed care and attention. More tests, more scary conditions to test for…my poor brain hurt at the thought of more. I supposed that I needed to be sure that there wasn't something wrong that needed fixing, but I wasn't happy about it!

Phil went back to work the following day and I got up late as I had been forbidden from going anywhere near The Witches Brew for a while yet. Within minutes of getting up and starting to walk around I had a familiar realisation, my arm was weak again and I couldn't properly feel my left leg. Once again I got on the phone to Phil Bryson, but there would be no more trips to Plymouth.

After the amount of recompression I had received I would gain no further benefits. How I was feeling would be the best I could expect. Diving bends usually get better on their own within 6-8 months. As long as the heart and lung tests came up clear I wouldn't need any more treatment apart from rest and of course no diving.

Hmm, this hadn't been the magic pill answer I had hoped for. I thought maybe there was a quick fix that a third visit would give, but apparently not. 6-8 months was a long time to go with a weak arm and pretend leg. After all I had a business to run and a life to lead.

I've had my share of challenges over the years and 13 years of personal development experience under my belt. I had learned that a great technique in times of stress was simply to put one foot in front of the other, to work step by step and gradually find your way. I decided that I would take the rest of the week to rest as I was told, but that work would resume on Monday.

One action that seemed very obvious to me though was to ask Ami to be Assistant Manager. She had coped admirably in my absence, keeping to schedules and preparing tick lists as well as keeping our regulars updated of my progress. I knew she had enjoyed it and would be an asset to our company.

Initially when we had worked together we clashed heads, the mix of my flowing nature and Ami's need for rules and regularity didn't always blend well. Some of our customers had raised eyebrows when we had impromptu debates in the shop about best practise and Ami refused to take 'because I said so' as a reason. Her logical and well researched suggestions meant that we were always improving techniques and finding time savers, something that had eluded me while trying to wear all the hats at once.

I didn't like to admit it, but I was feeling quite weak and shaky after recent events. I had always joked that I was Super Mummy, having been a single parent and business woman in equal measure. The adrenaline rush had subsided and left me feeling tired and I had yet to test the limits of my weakened arm and leg. I wondered how I would cope when I ventured back to normality. My new fledgling business had been a huge undertaking when I was 100% fit; I thought that perhaps there would need to be some changes to the plan in my current state.

8 LIFE CARRIES ON AT THE WITCHES BREW

Monday morning arrived and it felt very strange putting on my uniform cerise pink polo shirt. It was as if wearing this had happened in another lifetime, not just over a week ago. I wanted to reassure my customers that I was back to normal and that all was well, so added some extra make up for good measure. I knew I was also reassuring myself, but that was okay.

I got as far as the car before I encountered a problem. It seemed that my brain to foot co-ordination was having a malfunction. Clutch control was one of the easiest skills I had mastered when learning to drive and my hill starts were almost poetry in motion and yet now I couldn't make it past a junction without stalling. I didn't quite register the problem at first, driving is always such an automatic function, but after a while it dawned on me. How would I get to work if I couldn't drive my car?

My left arm was responsible for gear changing and this added another problem. The weakness I had meant changing gears, particularly from third gear back down to second was hard and my arm ached after being in the car for a short while. I battled on through the journey from North Common to Whitchurch, but there was profuse swearing along the way, and all the while my apprehension was building.

The Witches Brew was in a great location on the main A37 Wells Road out of town and the estimate was that 20,000 cars a day drove this route. Parking outside the shop was limited and so we parked opposite in the pub.

Once I had parked up and started to walk to the road I was acutely aware of the tingling, not quite there feeling in my leg. So far it had held my weight even though I had reduced sensations, but what if I was to fall while on that busy road? This wasn't the journey I had expected on my first day of trying to be super confident and bouncy! Instead I took my time, crossed further along on the pedestrian crossing and was quietly relieved to find Ami alone in the shop as my smile had most definitely slipped.

Over the following days I did my best to convince everyone it was business as normal. Of course I recounted the tale of my recent adventures, using artistic license to gloss over the serious longer term bits and embellishing my rescue by gorgeous maritime hunks. No-one knew that my journey to work involved numerous stalls, that my swear words had increased in magnitude and venom and that on bad days I rang Ami from my car so that she could watch me across the road and rescue me should I fall…

Any time I was tired my arm would act like a petulant child, refusing to follow the commands that my brain issued. My speech was affected too. Words would fail me at the instant I was about to use them and I would hunt around the recesses of my mind to quickly find an alternative. My shoulder was still painful and ached most of the time, getting coats on took a while and still gear changes sometimes had an accompanying wince.

Generally though I glossed over the challenges and set about proving that life carried on. After all, the effects would be temporary and so over time my body would heal itself and life could get back to normal. It was frustrating that this happened when I had so much to do, but now Ami was at my side we had double the time and double the brain power; each day we were finding new routines to streamline and prioritise.

There were constant reminders of my challenges and it was sometimes hard to acknowledge how much life had changed. I had a habit of moving rooms around on a whim or having a huge de-clutter, but found picking up boxes or moving furniture impossible. I had never been one to ask for help, but now I had no choice. Patience was also never a strong point; once I thought of it I wanted it done.

This could no longer happen, I simply had to wait. If I had ever had a cold or been under the weather I would get no sympathy from Phil who had only ever had a couple of days off in his life. Now though he would lift things for me without question and ask me how I was feeling. This would have been welcomed previously during a round of the sniffles, but this made me uneasy as it reminded me how serious life had got. Usually at home we made our own little bubble, work stayed at work and any challenges were always laughed about. Now it seemed the seriousness had penetrated our defences, there was no escaping the obvious.

Diving was such a large part of our world and we had a calendar full of trips planned that I could no longer join. I still went along to our club meetings on a Wednesday night and had been taken aback at how kind and concerned everyone was. So many of them had been on Lundy and had showed their concern first hand.

I smiled and reassured everyone that I was fine and would soon be back at sea. It did feel strange though, being somewhere with a focus on something that had not only completely changed my body but also that I would be unable to do for a while yet. Talking about it seemed to make my symptoms worse, as if the focus reminded me of how weak and aching I felt. After a couple of weeks I was glad to melt back into the group and talk about something else.

Our family has always had a secret defence to be wheeled out in times of adversity: humour. I came from a family of sarcastic folk, who could use wit and humour to dig themselves out of the most serious of situations. My brother and I had always laughed and joked growing up and my girls had taken our foundations to another level in recent years. Phil too, shared the sarcastic gene which was a relief!

Any family get together always had at least one instance of collapsing into tears of uncontrollable laughter. Usually one of us – and it could be anyone – would see a new joke in the words of the others and that would be it. The shoulders would start to shake, the tears would fall and they would be powerless to share their thoughts. It would take several minutes before they could share, by which time at least one other person if not more would also be crying with laughter, at the helplessness of the other.

This defence really came into its own now, as being serious only intensified my doubts and rippled worries from one day out into the next. I knew I had some testing times ahead what with keeping the shop going as well as the myriad of medical tests I had to go through. If I stayed serious I knew from past experience that my worries would get bigger and I would create dark, testing scenarios that would never happen in reality.

I started making fun of all my own shortcomings and asked everyone to follow. At the shop I would often have mishaps, either burning my numb little finger when steaming the milk, or thinking I had stopped pouring the milk into the cup only to be nudged by Ami who had spotted the milk still running down the draining board. "Get it together Mum!" she would laugh and the tension would drain from any scenario.

If anything needed lifting I would simply raise an eyebrow and look at Ami, "My crip hand won't lift that!" I would say and she would wear a pained expression, "Do I have to do everything these days?" Our laughter replaced any feelings of inadequacy with those of love for the family that surrounded me. I knew there had been times when I had carried them, from tiny babies needing everything through to some challenging years growing up. Here was my turn and I needed to accept help with grace and a smile; I could do that.

Our customers always asked how I was feeling and it was lovely to see such a firsthand example of the community we had created. I assured them I was fine, getting better each day. I was sure that if I kept telling myself this then it would naturally happen. I had read countless books of how our thoughts become things, of how what we focus on we get more of. I was not going to grumble and moan and list everything I couldn't do.

I carried on with my holistic treatments, giving Reiki, Indian Head Massage and Reflexology as normal. There were a few hiccups; my shoulder would ache and some Reflexology moves had to be fudged due to the limited shoulder movement. The hardest treatment was Indian Head massage, doing lymphatic drainage would see my right hand splayed into the position I had learned, whereas my left hand was a crumpled heap. I could still do the move but it was hard getting used to that sight. In my head I would take the image of my right hand and gently encourage my left to unfurl and adopt the same position.

I still took on the ethos of healer heal thyself and gratefully accepted offers of Reiki and other treatments. There was even a homeopathic remedy for

Decompression Injuries and taking it reduced the fizzing sensation in my arm.

Hot stone therapies enabled more movements in my limbs, although we had to be careful as I was unable to gauge the temperature of the stones laid on my left side. Cranial Osteopathy helped with my shoulder pain and also my co-ordination. It seemed as if my body had lost its map of what went where and how, but these sessions seemed to help.

I was so very grateful for the years of holistic therapy knowledge that I had and the network of amazing people I now knew. I had no help offered from the medical team, no physiotherapy or further information. I had years of training behind me, I had learned about the body, about the effects of stress and the positive benefits available from complementary therapy.

What would I have done if I hadn't known there were ways to help myself? I supposed I would have lived on painkillers and grumbling – I really did count myself lucky that I had another way of doing things.

I would often dream of being stuck in the kelp on the ocean bed, unable to free myself and get to the surface. The dreams were very vivid; I could feel the kelp on my face and the icy cold grip of the sea water. I would try to untangle myself but just get further wrapped up in the weed and murk. I would hear the sounds of the sea bed around me and wake in a breathless sweat.

I thought this was my subconscious way of expressing how I was feeling, as during my waking hours I wouldn't let myself give in to wallowing or any thought of not recovering. This was a temporary blip on a beautiful landscape, one to be glossed over rather than studied. I had more to accomplish in the next 40 years than I had in the previous 40 and this would not set me back.

9 PASTURES NEW

We had a dive trip planned for September that year, on St Mary's in the Isles of Scilly. It would feel strange going along and not diving while the rest of the group got up with the lark and excitedly headed to the quay. I loved the Scillies, with its beautiful beaches and friendly pubs and it would be great to get away and relax.

I was an expert at keeping up a jovial façade in the shop, even when some days I was aching and sore. I knew my ailments were temporary and so didn't want to complain anyway, but even I had to admit that life was more of a struggle these days and I got tired easily. It would be so nice to get a week of peace and quiet.

I had started writing a book the year before, a story based on my own journey from an unhappily married accountant to a liberated and happy psychic. It was based around a fictional character called Tabby and her fictional family. I felt strongly that it should be fiction rather than an autobiography as the aim of the book was to inspire others rather than talk about me. I decided that our holiday would be a great time to get more of the book done.

We were camping on a site away from the town, with a 20 minute uphill hike to the campsite. Each morning I would wave the divers off and enjoy a quiet cuppa before heading to civilisation. The campsite was a quiet nature haven, with deer, a robin, a family of inquisitive blackbirds and a gaggle of cheeky sparrows that would scavenge for crumbs in your tent if you left a zip undone! It was here that I could just be, I could sit and watch the natural world for half an hour without feeling the call of a to-do list.

After a misty start the sun came out each day just in time for the walk to town. I was armed with a laptop and notebook and developed a great routine in the first couple of days. I chose some great eateries - Kavorna for the morning and Woodcock and Mumford for the afternoon. Coffee followed by hot chocolate and the odd lemonade with a delicious piece of quiche to keep me going at lunch.

Even though the book was a fiction the experiences I was drawing upon contained some harsh memories and some days the tears would flow as I quietly tapped away on the keyboard. Those years had been awash with challenge, bereavements and heart wrenching decisions, life threats and feelings of powerlessness. Years had gone by and life had changed for the better but it was as if it was all happening there and then once I started to write.

It was often a relief when it was time to re-join reality and the divers, with their happy tales of diving depths and funny kit mishaps. We had a great group of people, all intent on being safe while having fun. Sunny afternoons were spent on the terrace of the Atlantic pub, often with a game of cards and a cold lager.

The week was a great mix of morning cathartic storytelling and afternoon social encounters. It was great to see Phil diving with the group. He had been a little cautious knowing that I was confined to barracks, but once he realised I enjoyed my writing challenge he could enjoy his holiday. I knew that diving was his life passion and it made me smile seeing his happy face greet me each afternoon.

It was a little concerning that I wouldn't be diving with him. We had always checked on each other and developed an almost symbiotic relationship, instinctively knowing how the other was feeling. Now I would have to entrust that to someone else.

I knew he was highly trained and methodical and always took care, checking everything off before each dive. I knew that our club's motto was Cavendo Tutus: Safety Through Caution and that the ethos was practiced throughout the club. I knew that my bend was out of the ordinary and rare…but it didn't stop me worrying about the man I loved. A small part of me held my breath until I got the text saying they were in the pub!

At the end of the week I had 9,000 words written which was around a third of my target, with a good plan of how I would complete the rest. I didn't have a publishing date in mind; I would take my time and wait until I was happy with my draft before sending it out to my waiting spellcheckers.

I felt that rather than spending the week in limbo listening to other people's experiences I had crafted one of my own. My first book had been a compilation of one hundred tips, useful but not really a literary work of art. I loved that it was out helping people, but this next book was my step into that of a writer, which was exciting and daunting all at once. I imagined the book launch, similar to those we held at The Witches Brew sharing snippets and answering questions. I was excited at the prospect and wondered what the reaction to it would be.

As autumn drew the nights in and added a frosty edge to the mornings the aches in my shoulder and arm increased. I was concerned that there were no outward signs of recovery, in fact I felt like I was going backwards. Often I would be kept awake at night by the pain in my arm and shoulder. I would tussle with pillows trying to find a comfortable spot, but there didn't seem to be one.

The sensation was like toothache, nagging, gnawing and constant. The hours between 2am and 5am were the worst and quite often I gave up, tiptoeing downstairs to catch up on some marketing or admin over a cup of coffee. Phil was no longer surprised to find me here wrapped up in a dressing gown looking grumpy when he got up at 5am to head for work. Sometimes I would try to get another couple of hours once he left, but I fancied I felt worse getting up a second time. Most weekday mornings I went networking to drum up business for The Witches Brew and would just pile on the makeup and ensure the coffee kept flowing.

The sofa at the shop became my best friend when we had evening events. I would close the shop at 4pm, tidy up and then grab an hour of snoozing before our next guests arrived. I had always been able to cat nap, setting an alarm and curling up. These days though it was a necessity not a luxury; my disturbed sleep at night time meant I couldn't last a whole day without a catch up.

On particularly bad days it was hard to keep up the smiles and sunny disposition I had become known for. Ami and I would sit down with a hot chocolate to plan our day and she would do her utmost to share the load. I would write my list and she would go through it taking some of the tasks to do. She was very pragmatic and adept at rallying me, "Look Mum, we know this is temporary don't we? Let me help for now and soon you'll be back to 100%. We're in it together, don't worry."

Of course she was right, the divers I had spoken to who had suffered the bends had corroborated the advice given by DDRC. They had been better within 6-8 months and were symptom free and back to diving. It was hard for now but it would pass and I wanted to keep battling through. So our list would be shared, we would end up giggling and by the time we opened the doors my smile was back.

I was now a regular at our local hospitals as the ruling out process began. My first visit was to check for a hole in my heart at Frenchay hospital. I wasn't quite sure what I wanted the result to be; a positive result would give me a reason for my bend, but then would I want heart surgery to go diving again? A hole free heart would be the best news, but then more tests would ensue to find the cause.

The procedure was undertaken by a lovely doctor and nurse who explained every step. A cannula was inserted into my arm and my heart was monitored on a scan. I was asked to hold my breath while saline was injected into my bloodstream. Eagerly I watched the screen – a hole would mean we would see the saline leaking between ventricles. After repeating the process, it was clear – no hole.

Next I went off to Cossham hospital to visit a lung specialist and more tests were ordered. Again, nothing was found except a lowered lung function due to the recent decompression injury.

So I had no reason for my symptoms. No magic pill to take to make it all go away. It appeared that I was one of the 40% who never found a reason for their bend. Despite my wish to find a good reason why, I just had to wait it out and see what happened next. My inner control freak grumbled and growled at this outcome, but I had no choice, there was nothing left to test.

10 FINDING A CAUSE

It was now January 2011; six months had passed since our Lundy trip. My symptoms and pain were now more pronounced than ever, with my nights more sleepless and painful than ever. It seemed there was no end in sight and I was persuaded back to the GP by my Mum who referred me to a consultant neurologist at Frenchay hospital.

Mum came with me for my appointment and we chatted about what he would say in the waiting room. We concluded that maybe it was just taking longer than planned to recover; after all I was still running a business six days a week.

My consultant was a lovely man, I was guessing in his late thirties or early forties. I explained what had happened so far and the tests I had undergone, as well as the constant pain in residence in my arm. He wrote lots of notes and asked a few questions before beginning his examinations.

Sitting up on the couch he began poking and prodding. I was to answer whether I felt the pin to be soft or sharp as he alternated between the pin's point and its rubber covered head. He worked his way down my right side and the answers were clear – I felt I would have got 100% of the correct responses.

When it was the turn of my left side my answers surprised even me. There was numbness not only in my arm and leg, but it seemed that my face and the whole of my left side were quite numb. The weakness in my arm and leg was still very pronounced too. Of course I hadn't had any reason to test these things myself since my visit to DDRC in July. The shock must have showed on my face as I noticed my Mum's tearful look of concern.

He concluded that my injuries were either down to nitrogen bubbles on my spinal cord or a stroke caused by bubbles in the brain. When I recounted my visual disturbances at the time, inability to recall facts and subsequent memory loss he thought it had been a stroke. It appeared the damage had been in the Thalamus, the part of the brain responsible for motor skills and sensations.

Stroke. Aged 40 I had suffered a stroke. This wasn't a temporary bend where my symptoms would just disappear. How I was feeling, my pain and weakness was caused by a stroke; nitrogen bubbles rather than a bleed, but a stroke nonetheless. Permanent damage to the tissues in my brain.

I asked what happened next: nothing. My motor skills weren't severely damaged and so physiotherapy wasn't needed. How I was feeling in eighteen months time would be how I would stay. Any recovery I got in that time would be the maximum I could expect.

Mum and I left in silence and walked back to the car. My foot scuffed the floor as my symptoms shouted out louder than ever. I could sense a flood of words and questions stirring in my head but they were behind a brick wall, unable to escape. For now, we made our way home and did what we did best: we put the kettle on.

Suddenly there was permanence to my condition. No temporary blip on the landscape, rather a long-term condition etching into the future that needed to be planned around. This was a long term prognosis that required long term decisions and grown up ones at that. What would I do about the shop? What about this year's dive trips that were now an impossibility? How about my driving? Temporary stalling on my journey to work required swearing and huffing, but I couldn't do this permanently. So many questions were building up but all I could think of was one word: stroke.

When Phil arrived home I told him, as if you would share an item on the news. It hadn't sunk in yet, but I figured if I got used to saying it aloud then it would gradually become my reality. Phil's face told me that I was right to be asking all of these questions, he didn't shrug it off or make a joke. He stood and listened intently, taking in every word and detail. I didn't tell anyone else that day; I needed my bubble of mindless TV and the comfort of a shared bottle of wine.

I suddenly felt as if I was made of eggshell, fragile and in need of care and attention. Just the mention of the word stroke had made my pain more intense, my weakness more pronounced and my mental capacity dwindle. It was one, short word and yet it had a magnitude I couldn't quite comprehend. Nothing had changed after my visit to the neurologist. I was the same as before, I just had more knowledge.

Over the following days I had conversations with family and friends. I was so grateful for the love and support I knew I had around me. We could swing between heartfelt sympathy, serious advice, and general chit chat while the tears fell. We would always somehow get back to a lighter conversation and end on a giggling note of hilarity.

The consensus among my nearest and dearest was that no-one would blame me if I gave up the shop, after all I hadn't banked on a stroke when I started out. They would all help to sort it out with me. If, however I wanted to keep going they would be behind me all the way.

We had worked so hard, created so much and were only at the beginning of our journey. To stop now seemed so final. I had Ami by my side and my family behind me; I decided to carry on for now and to see what unfolded, life was a journey after all.

The more people I told, the more I accepted and got used to the word stroke. As one day blended into another life carried on. Still the pain continued, but it had become a known friend now. I accepted the sleepless nights as normal now and knew what would hurt and what wouldn't. I had always balked at routine when being an accountant, wishing to be out on the road varying my work. Yet here I was, six days a week plodding on a treadmill in unconscious fashion. I began to resist new ideas and hang on to the same old same old. What was known seemed safe.

February arrived with a chilly fanfare and I headed off for our annual ski holiday, a week in the mountains of Sauze D'Oux along with Phil and a group of friends. We were mixed abilities, from the competent and elegant black run skiers, through the red run riders ending with me – the slow coach at the back. I had taken to the skiing lifestyle like a duck to water. I had always found peace and clarity from being at altitude among the beautiful, snow capped peaks.

The actual skiing came a little harder, discovering a gripping fear of falling over the edges of the tracks carved into the mountains. My early years had involved lots of crying, crazy nightmares of constantly falling off cliffs and what seemed like hours being frozen to the spot on the slopes in a blind panic. Some hypnotherapy had taken the fear away, but getting the knack of anything harder than a snow plough had taken a while longer…several years in fact! My nickname was the Racing Snail and I could be seen daily traversing the nursery slopes with my bottom sticking out and a determined expression.

I loved so much about skiing that I was going to crack it, and eventually something clicked. I progressed from blue to red and even managed the odd black run these days as long as it was wide and Phil had done a practise run first. This time I took a very sedentary approach, sticking to easy blue runs and nipping off for hot chocolate breaks at regular intervals. In a big group there was always someone who wanted a rest and Phil - my kamikaze husband who loved to throw himself down as many runs as possible – always found some fellow crazies to play with.

This year though I had a few new challenges to ski with. It was a little tricky at first; my left leg was not as responsive as my right and I had a lesson to learn some extra techniques to make turning easier. My hand and arm ached more at night from carrying skis and poles and I gratefully accepted my husband's offers of help. Again the rule of 'if you can't carry it you shouldn't be doing it' had been temporarily forgotten and replaced with a smile and a wink.

We had a great week, activity by day and good food and conversation by night. There were no injuries either; I had clocked up a few over the years as I tried to conquer this alien sport. This time I didn't even fall off the ski lift, something I had become famous for!

Once we got home and settled back into working life I did something empowering that perhaps should have been done before; I went to the

Citroen dealership and replaced my current manual C1 with a new, shiny automatic version. The profanity filled journeys and painful gear changing would soon be a thing of the past. It seemed like one obvious step towards making my life simpler.

I had always changed my car on a whim, deciding at breakfast and signing the deal before teatime, so this wasn't really a huge move for me. It did however signal a start of the adjustments that I would need to make to look after myself in the days to come.

As the dive season started up there was the usual fervour of planning trips and checking which weekends were the most favourable. We always tried for the first week in April and this year was no exception. I decided to go along for the ride, thinking that a weekend by the sea would be a good excuse for a chill.

Although I still felt guilty turning my back on the shop I recognised that always working was what had got me into my current situation. We had taken on some temporary staff now, wonderful ladies who would come in for the odd day when we needed some helping hands.

Jemima was our crystal expert, always smiling and willing to go the extra mile for our customers. I always knew when Jemima had been in, the plants would be watered and our stock of crystals and jewellery would be sparkling. She would take them all out; give them a polish and a cuddle before carefully placing them back into their glass cabinet at a new jaunty angle. Interestingly our crystal sales always went up after Jemima had called!

Jacqui helped us on Wednesdays and would always bounce in with a smile. I had never met someone with so much energy! Her routine involved several exercise classes, walks, helping her elderly aunt and a full social calendar. She was meticulous with her cleaning and so again I would know when Jacqui had been working – we could never get the stainless quite as sparkling as Jacqui could.

Zoe was another fantastic addition, we had been friends for years through the dive club and Zoe brought her creative talents to our shop. Over her time with us beautiful bunting appeared, fantastic hand crafted ornaments and a beautiful painted tree adorned our front window for a while which really captured attention!

These wonderful people meant I could take that weekend away and join in on the dive trip ahead. Our car was packed full of dive and camping kit as we set off for Plymouth. We collected the club RHIB on the way down - we kept it at a farm in Portishead so it didn't take long to hitch it up and get back on the road. We pitched our tent in the sunshine before wandering off to the pub.

Our favourite campsite had been carefully selected, not too far from Queen Anne Battery where we launched the boat, within walking distance of the pub and of course the fish and chip shop. The showers were hot and there was plenty of room for whoever came along, depending on whether there was one boat or two we could need most of the lower field.

Early the next morning everyone was up assembling their kit and loading their cars. I had nothing to do except stand and watch with my coffee. This felt very alien to me as usually you had an eye on your watch while you quickly got everything done, no-one wanted to be the last one to leave. We always had a definite ropes off time and as the tide didn't wait we needed to be ready…this morning however I had no sense of urgency.

I felt uncomfortable in my own skin; I was no longer part of the crowd. I had been taken out of the world I knew so well and hadn't planned for what would replace it. I wasn't a diver and wouldn't ever be, I knew all the vocabulary but couldn't join in any more. I braved a smile and told Phil that I had decided to chill at the campsite. We had an electric hook-up and I had my laptop, I would get on with my book for a bit and enjoy the sunshine.

I waved everyone off and wished them a good day before going back to bed. I was literally a fish out of water and decided sleep would switch this feeling off for now. So much had changed and I had taken it all in my stride, yet here was something else to throw me off kilter.

I woke to find the sun shining and after a hot shower I felt a lot better. I fired up my trusty little laptop and wrote a few more chapters, writing took me into my own world. I had a playlist of my favourite tunes and hours passed, broken only by another cup of coffee and quick stretch. I curled up with a book in the afternoon – wherever I went I always took a selection 'just in case'.

By the time the divers came back, rosy from the wind and sun and bristling with tales of dogfish encounters, I was in much better spirits and happy to hear all the chatter. Phil looked relaxed and happy, if a little jaded from all the kit carrying and dive planning. He and Graeme were well known in the club for their meticulous planning and perfectly timed weekends, but I knew the effort this took on their parts.

We headed off to the pub and took our time choosing from the scrumptious menu of The Foxhound, they always had so much to offer and of course we needed to leave room for ice-cream! We sleepily plodded home with a full tummy and a warm fuzzy feeling brought on by 2 glasses of wine.

The spring evenings were chilly so we quickly tucked up in our sleeping bags covered with thermals and hoodies. I had learned from my first trip with Phil that, "There is no such thing as bad weather, just wrong clothes." and so gave up glamour in favour of warmth and comfort!

The next morning, I joined in the scrabble. We were heading home straight after the afternoon dive and so our tent had to be packed up – after regulation bacon butties of course! We had a routine that had evolved over many trips: I would pack up the inside of the tent while Phil cooked. He would then dismantle the tent while I washed up (wiped the pan over with kitchen roll). Soon we were off to find the boat, check her over and prepare for another day.

Again as everyone grappled with kit and wriggled their way into under-suits and dry suits I had that lost feeling. I went off to find takeaway coffees, determined to be useful. I did try to lend a hand and carry some kit, but most dive kit required two handed efforts and I only had one that would grip. Today I had a car for company and the sunshine had been replaced by rain. I found some business development CDs that I had packed in my work bag and set about inspiring my mind.

I wandered off in search of lunch and spent a couple of hours in a local greasy spoon café with my laptop. I enjoyed a sandwich and several mugs of milky coffee before I felt like I was outstaying my welcome. I headed back to the car, thinking that I would have to find more to do on weekends like these. Doing nothing was hard to do when the rest of your life revolved around action. I had spent years multi-tasking while working and bringing up my girls and the last year had been full of Witches Brew activities. When I had nothing to do my brain would start going over the things it couldn't do – and I had no time for that.

11 DARK DAYS

Dropping the shower head was the last straw. Something snapped inside and the tears started to roll. No shouting, no outward flash, just a silent giving up that had been a long time coming. Through my tears I got dressed, went downstairs and rang my Dad. "I dropped the shower. I won't be coming into work today." I managed to croak between sniffs and long silences holding back the tears. "Don't worry my love, I'll get Mum to come over." This was the reply of a man well used to dealing with his daughter!

I made myself a cup of coffee and sat on the sofa – somewhere I never sat these days as I was either at the coffee shop working or using the kitchen table as my personal office. I stayed on the sofa with the blackout blinds down, in a daze and completely shut off. It appeared the numbness was here to stay – my usual sparking, creative, idea a minute brain had abandoned me. Here it was: defeat.

I had battled the pain and insomnia for about five months and refused to give in. Every day I got up after my usual couple of hours sleep. Sometimes I got up through the night and worked for a bit, other times I lay in the dark fidgeting and hoping not to disturb Phil. Bit by bit though, my energy had ebbed away and the pain etched into my face. Gradually tiredness had been silently replaced by exhaustion and my body started to buckle.

I snapped myself out of the fog long enough to call the doctor, as I knew this is where my mum would take me when she arrived. Usually I refused any of these visits preferring home remedies or a holistic approach, but the last few months had been an endless round of hospitals, tests and follow ups so I was almost immune by now. In my numb apathy the path of least resistance seemed my only option.

Mum arrived with a balance of concern and steely resolve. "Don't you worry my love, we'll get this sorted. There are things we can do, let's get you to the doctors." I usually had a witty response, a sarcastic phrase to make light of any situation. Today, I had nothing. I managed a weak smile through the latest wave of tears and that was as much as I could muster.

The doctor raised an eyebrow as the blood pressure monitor read 171/103. Our family had a history of high blood pressure with both Mum & Dad taking medication. I knew these numbers were too high and so didn't object to the request for bed rest and quiet – I welcomed it in fact. I felt like a fragile, ticking time bomb, I had burning cheeks and a flutter in my chest as well as an inability to think.

My mum was amazing, whisking me off home and rallying with cups of tea and coffee. She kept the conversation to easy, light chit chat and shared frequent quick hugs – not too long as past experience had taught her that this started the tears again.

The maternal line in our family have all been strong, capable women and well used to dropping everything and wading in when help is needed. On this particular day I was very grateful. I went back to the sofa and watched the world go by.

When Phil arrived home he took one look and realised something had changed. "I gave up." I said simply and that was enough. He had watched week on week as I paced the house by night and sighed by day. Of course at work my smile was painted on, but the magic of our marriage was that I could always just be myself. Phil had a way of knowing how I was feeling without me needing to say a word. I remember on our second date he had looked deep into my eyes and remarked how there were so many emotions hiding behind my smile. At the time I had been shocked – how could this man I had only just met know me better than previous partners, who had either not seen or just weren't looking?

As the day drew to a close I moved my behind from the sofa to the kitchen chair. Phil and Mum chatted away about work and the family as if nothing was happening. Another steaming mug of coffee was passed to me and I almost felt as if life was pretty normal.

After three days of darkness, duvet rest and brainless days I returned to the doctor. This time both eyebrows were raised: 192/110, a new record. The feelings of a fluttering heart, general weakness, flushed hot cheeks and a racing kind of panic were more present than ever so I didn't flinch at the suggestion of the pills that I usually avoided like the plague.

In fact, "In for a penny, in for a pound." I thought and shared the unending pain and sleeplessness that had been torturing me for months. I left with a prescription for blood pressure medication and heavy duty painkillers, as well as a strange feeling of relief.

Apart from the occasional course of antibiotics and the odd fad of vitamin taking I had never been on regular medication. The blood pressure medication was to be taken each morning and the painkillers every twelve hours. It was probably a placebo effect that already I was feeling better after the first blood pressure tablet, however there was no doubt when the painkillers started to work.

Initially there were waves of nausea and my stomach churned when I tried to eat. As the effects of the medication built up I developed a dull headache and my head felt like it was filled with cotton wool. A friend warned me of the side effects and I had always needed small doses of any medication, but this reaction knocked me sideways!

But – the pain was no more. My nights were filled with deep, uninterrupted sleep, as were large chunks of my days. My arm didn't throb, my shoulder was pain free too and the fluttering in my chest had stopped. It seemed as if someone had turned my body to its hibernate setting and I was eternally grateful.

My Tarot cards had always been by my side in times of transition and this time was no different. One morning after the fog had lifted a little I shuffled the cards and picked one: the ten of swords. This card meant rock bottom. There was nowhere else to fall, no lower to go, from this point onwards the only way was up. I remembered a phrase that JK Rowling had used: rock bottom became the solid foundation from which I rebuilt my life. I felt that this was where I was residing; rock bottom.

I looked back over my recent past. May last year I was working full steam ahead, filled with enthusiasm and passion. I had forgotten all about myself, of staying strong by nurturing my body, maintaining a balanced work ethic and keeping my spirits high through meditation and time spent in nature. On and on I had gone, trying to squeeze more into my days and more out of my body – had I not learned from past experiences that this approach didn't work?

Even after my bend I was driven to show everyone that I was ok. I had appeared to bounce back and carried on with life at one hundred miles an hour. Always trying to do something new, invent a new strategy and take on as much responsibility as possible. Even when I wasn't sleeping I still dashed off to networking meetings and manned our evening events too.

Until now when I had nothing left to give. No reserves of energy to pull on. My mental capacity was zero; concentration lasted a few minutes at the most. I was more tired than I could ever remember and needed to retire to the warmth of my duvet at least four times a day. I would still be heading for bed by 9pm to sleep the whole night.

When I finally took a good, hard and honest look in the mirror I could see the dark circles and the years that continuous pain had added to my features. My hair was lank and lifeless and the sparkle that often got mistaken for flirting that was just my love of life was completely extinguished.

If I carried on this way what would be next? Already I had suffered a stroke; at what point did the body give up completely? I was 41 years old; my children were 20 and 17. I had only just found my soul mate six years earlier; did I not want to see how this played out?

I knew the answer deep down; of course I did. I needed to take some time, to just breathe, to rest and to heal. For now I would accept that I needed help, that I was in a broken state and had no idea what to do next, but that was okay. I had worked through times in my life where the plan had gone out of the window, I could do it again.

I was surrounded by amazing and wonderful family and friends. I had an awesome marriage. I had cute and magical cats always ready to play. We had a nice if a little chaotic home to live in. I had both my parents, something that I valued highly. I had my own business and was in the lucky position of being able to take some time off. I had a laptop so could assist and plan from home.

I also had a secret weapon. I had fourteen years behind me of crafting my intuition and a wealth of holistic knowledge. Through running events I had a group of contacts that practised every form of holistic therapy I could imagine. I had learned personal development strategies and heard of life changes from some of the top gurus in the UK and America. In my cupboards I had piles of notebooks filled with tips, techniques, action plans and inspiration.

I had learned to walk my talk, to take responsibility for my actions. I knew that I could choose what happened next and immerse myself in positivity and nurturing. Okay, I had wobbled away from my chosen path, but now was the perfect time to change that. The past had already been written, but who said my future should go the way of the victim?

The medication was a wonderful relief and giving my body the crutch it needed, but I knew how incredible our innate healing abilities were. With time, planning, patience and loving care I could change my current state. This project was bigger than anything I had worked towards before, but I could just take one step and one day at a time and see where I ended up!

12 BACK TO BASICS

The next day I asked Mum to take me to visit The Witches Brew. I had been away for a while and so much had happened, it felt very strange to be going to the shop with no plan of work. I called Ami, Jemima and Jacqui together and asked for their help. If I was going to get my strength back I would need to take some time out. I couldn't guarantee being there regularly and we had a full schedule of events planned for the summer – would they be able to step in and cover me?

Their responses, smiles and extra ideas made me heave a sigh of relief. I was so blessed to have a team like this working with me. Easily they planned their time around all the events and an action plan was hatched for the coming month as well as a review meeting to check our progress.

I was only allowed an hour sitting with a cup of tea before I was shooed off home – they had it covered, I didn't need to worry.

So now I could focus on getting myself back to fighting fit. The blood pressure medication had worked its magic and my last check had made the doctor happy – 120/80, perfectly normal. For now I would carry on with the tablets, but I had the doctor's promise – at such a point where my blood pressure was normal and stable I could stop taking the tablets and he would support me. I had got to know my own GP quite well and it turned out he was a diver too!

The Gabapentin that I was taking were huge, horse-sized pills and provided 24 hour pain relief. They also provided 24 hour a day nausea, foggy brain

and a horrible taste in my mouth. They had given me welcome relief from
my lively aches and pains, but I couldn't drive, work or even think while
taking them – there had to be an alternative.

I had been given a book by Vanessa, one of my customers, called Your
Mind Can Heal Your Body by Dr David Hamilton. She had read it and
found it very valuable with her own health challenges. I began to read and
found piece after piece of valuable information. The book was a mix of
science and positive thinking, talking about the placebo effect and the art of
visualising yourself well. There was a lot of detail about neural pathways
and how negative or damaged pathways can be replaced with new ones
using positive thought and visualising.

I had used visualising a lot in my psychic and Mediumship training but had
never tried it with my body. According to the book every cell in the body
was completely replaced every seven years. All were replaced at different
speeds, for example the cells on our eyes replace every two hours. It
seemed that each new cell carried a memory of the last, so if an old cell was
damaged the new one would come in with the same capacity – unless we
changed our thinking.

It was reading these words that I made a momentous decision: I would knit
myself a new arm! I started to think of my existing arm, with its weak
muscles and numbness through my little and ring fingers. I imagined
golden, vibrant nerve threads, weaving out from my chest through my
shoulder. In my mind's eye I would see each thread branching out into finer
and finer branches until the tips of each reached down to the tips of each
finger. As I watched each thread became brighter and brighter, glowing
with a brilliant golden hue. I imagined this golden light healing and
strengthening, evaporating away any pain and replacing it with vitality.

I practised this exercise several times a day, not with any particular intention
but just enjoying the process. I would feel clearer headed after doing this
and very relaxed too. For the first time in weeks or perhaps even months I
felt as if I was taking control back. I had accepted the diagnosis, the tests
and the treatment and for good reason. Now however, it was my turn to
take the driving seat and it felt good to be taking positive action.

I practised finger movements often too, watching my adept right hand and spurring my left to mimic. I practised clicking my fingers and glossed over the lack of sound. I practised my Indian Head Massage moves on myself too – enjoying the therapy as well as imagining my hands looking the same. Again it wasn't the results I focused on but the activity.

One of our therapists in the shop, Louise Morgan had just qualified in Aromatology. This was the science of using neat oils in treatment directly to the skin. It differed from using blends of oils in a carrier oil like almond oil for massage. This technique involved blending several neat oils for their healing qualities and then either drenching the skin or taking them internally. Louise had seen some amazing results while studying, including successfully treating MRSA, something that traditional medicine found a challenge.

I asked Louise if she could help me with my pain: even if I could just reduce the dose of my heavy duty painkillers this would be a start. We had great fun at the shop – Louise mixed a blend of oils for pain relief, tissue repair and relaxation. She applied sixty drops of neat oil to my arm and ten drops to each foot after heating the skin with a hairdryer to allow for easier osmosis. She then wrapped me in cling film and asked me to keep the wonderful smelling mix on for at least forty five minutes.

After the first treatment I was able to drop my daytime medication and remain pain free. Two more treatments and I stopped my painkillers completely. The pain did not return. I was amazed, relieved and elated at this wonderful treatment. Three treatments had completely relieved a constant, nagging and awful pain that I had lived with for so long and then masked with pills rich in side effects.

I was still looking after myself and resisted the temptation to start doing more work. However it was wonderful to think again and get my appetite back. I did worry at first that the relief would be temporary and was on guard for any twinges, but none came.

I had a weekly hot stone massage with our other Louise – Louise Alley. Each week she worked on smoothing out the knots in my muscles, sometimes adding in icy cold stones too. Gradually the movement in my shoulder increased and my hand felt more flexible.

I had monthly massages with Jemima too, determined to immerse myself in the healing properties of various therapies. Initially she had commented how the muscles in my left leg felt sponge like and unresponsive. This was stark contrast to my leg before my accident, 12 years of ballet, tap and modern dance as well as my recent pole dance instructor training had meant very defined leg muscles!

Now however she noticed a gradual improvement, each time my leg muscles took on a firmness and became defined once again. It was great to see such a visible sign of progress.

In May I had given up, feeling as if I had nowhere to go and nothing to give. On 26th July 2011, exactly one year after our trip to Lundy I had recovered 90% of the feeling and movement in my left side. In just two months my blood pressure had gone from raising the roof to consistently normal and I was completely pain free.

There was still the 10% to work on: I had weakness and limited use of my hand, my grip was diminished and my fingers stubbornly did their own thing. I had to assess lifting anything and remember to ask for help when it was needed. If I overdid it and worked too hard the aches would re-appear to remind me it was early days.

However, my memory was sharp once again and my speech now normal. I could feel my face and my smile was balanced once more. I was so happy to be seeing all the positive improvements I didn't really stop to think on how quickly this had happened. I was keen to stay on the positive path I had discovered and I also to see how far I could take this.

My attention was firmly fixed on each day, on the people around me and what I needed to do in that moment. Pre-accident my mind was always wandering into a panic about the future and trying to remember future tasks. Looking back it was as if I was haunted by my future which had put a huge strain on life – I had been unable to concentrate on anything but work. This of course had stolen my peace of mind and my present – I hadn't really enjoyed anything as it happened as I was pre-occupied with what was coming next. I had given half of my attention to most things, refusing to relax into anything as I was taunted by what was to come.

13 EVERYDAY LIFE

The last few months had highlighted the beautiful family I had around me and there were hours of smiles and happiness as we spent more time together. August brought even more happy times, Kassi returned from holiday with an engagement ring on her finger and Ami's partner Tom moved down from Leicester to live with her. It warmed my heart to watch my girls happy and growing up.

Ami, Kassi and Tom were all frequently at the Witches Brew and on one particular Friday that was a really good thing! I had been teaching Tarot all day and we had remarked on the rain that had persistently fallen the whole day. At 4pm my Tarot student left and we closed the shop, enjoying a final cuppa before we got soaked on the way home.

It was then that Ami asked if Tom could have some Reiki as he had never experienced it and had hurt his ankle. As Tom led on the couch I did my usual routine of asking him to close his eyes and relax. "Imagine lying on a sunny beach Tom, with the waves lapping at the shore." As I said these words I looked down to see water - real water – flooding the room from under the wall!

The drains behind our shop could no longer deal with the torrent of rainwater and so the back yard had flooded completely. Even though we had a high step into the shop this had been no match for the rising water. We all grabbed towels and tried to stop the flow of water into the shop, but soon realised there was no stopping this tide! All we could do was watch as the water level rose…if it carried on the kitchen cupboards would be full too.

"We need a bloody miracle!", I said to the girls and Tom…right before I saw the blue flashing lights of the fire brigade! Within minutes they had cleared the drain system and the water level stopped rising. They promised to come back and pump out the water once they had cleared the more urgent tasks.

We had been frantically lifting everything we could up on to tables and worktops and our efforts didn't stop there. I thought we should just sit and wait for the firemen to come back, but Ami, Tom and Kassi set to work with pint glasses and a bucket, literally bailing us out. Initially I thought this wouldn't work – but it's amazing what determination will do. They kept going, glass after glass and bucket after bucket, even though I couldn't see the progress and suggested they stop. Their hard work eventually started to show and kept the water away from the kitchen area. It stopped the floodwater soaking into the partition walls and our beautiful tongue and groove counter…probably saving us thousands on the repair bill.

When the firemen returned we were in much higher spirits and passed round the tea and cakes, they needed eating up as we would be closed for a while! Of course there were photos taken for our Facebook page – we always liked to share and our fire crew gave us big smiles!

Once home we all collapsed on the sofas and ordered pizza – there would be no cooking tonight! There was a real sense of team effort, we were surprisingly cheery considering the circumstances.

Later I talked to Phil who was in America with work and the enormity of the clean up job became apparent. Insurance, repair work, re-decoration and this on top of what was already a busy schedule…it was a daunting task and I asked myself if I was up to it. I wondered if this was a sign to stop, to give it all up and do something else. Could I really start again?

As usual I decided to take one step at a time and see where we ended up! I made a big list of everything to do and tried not to add my name beside everything. I tried to trust that somehow it would all get done.

The Facebook pictures had got an enormous response, with offers of help and messages of support. Our good friends Zoe and Dave were on site first thing the next morning, helping to lift the sodden wooden floors and carpets. A networking contact put a call in to a man with a van and on Sunday morning he loaded up and all the debris had been cleared.

By Monday we had dehumidifiers in place and within two days – even without a floor – we re-opened with a 'Phoenix from the flames' party. All of our regulars came in to say hello and lend their support.

One by one the challenges were dealt with. Eventually the insurance came through and we chose a beautiful new floor that gave the shop a real sparkle. We had a new and improved place to work in – although I would have chosen a more straightforward route to do it had I the choice!

This episode had been another huge challenge, but this time I had learned a lesson; to ask for help and work at a pace that didn't mean falling into a heap afterwards. I also didn't need all the answers to make a start; I needed to know what to do but not the how. My way of working was definitely changing – the old me would have spent hours working through scenarios and trying to do everything alone.

Over the next few months I kept asking for help when I needed it and continued to focus on my health. I was getting better at keeping my workload at a steady pace and watched out for tired patches. If I started to overdo anything my hand would ache, like a nagging, gnawing pain that could not be ignored. When I was too tired words would fail me too, my balance would deteriorate and I would snag my hip on a table edge.

The body knows that pain is a great reminder; nothing keens the senses more than a jangled nerve or aching fingers. I never worked through any of these pains; I would either take five and sit with a cuppa or scrap the list completely and start fresh the next day. I became able to gauge my body, know my limits and to work out which tasks suited what time of day.

Gradually something else happened – I stopped being a work bore! I realised that my whole life had revolved around The Witches Brew, its past, its present and its future. In my panic everything else had got squeezed out, including the people I loved.

Of course this had been for a very good reason – I wanted to build security for my family. I wanted to support my husband when the day came that he wanted to retire. I wanted to be able to easily pay when my girls decided to get married. I wanted to take my parents on wonderful holidays or indulge them in exciting treats. I wanted to take breaks with my friends and have time away to giggle.

All of this was wonderful – but if the cost had been my life, would any of them want these luxuries? Did I really have to set the bar so high that my very life had to be threatened before I would stop being my own awful taskmaster? Who was I trying to impress? What was I trying to prove?

I could only go back to the day I decided to leave my first husband and the promise I had silently made to my girls. My parents had always made me feel safe and I never had any awareness of when money was tight. I didn't want my children to suffer one moment of angst due to the choices that I made.

Of course I made my choices with their highest good at heart and it had taken literally years for me to be brave enough to leave. I had struck out on my own, built a new home and kept everything together. We had grown together as a unit of three and despite some tears there had been laughter and fun most of the time. Underneath all of it though there had been a warrior lioness, ever watchful and guarding her cubs, striving to be the best mum and provider.

Once I knew we would survive it seemed I had set my sights higher. My parents had been amazing throughout my divorce, helping out with their time, their money and most of all their love, ensuring my girls knew how special they were. Of course no thanks were needed but I wanted to show how much I appreciated them. I wanted to treat them so they could see that what they did was special.

When I met Phil he had become the best male friend that my girls could have. He made them laugh, he stayed relaxed and calm in a crisis and he gave the best fashion advice – ever! He had blended into our family in such an easy way, always putting my tribe ahead of himself and had never made one demand in return.

I had continued to love this man more and more each day and so of course I wanted to look after him the way he had looked after me.

No-one had asked for anything in return. No-one had specified that they were only helping if they got something back. None of these people even knew they were on my 'indulgence hit list' and if they had, they would have dismissed it all in an instant!

Yet here I had been striving away, with my honourable future plans chipping away at me. I had to come to terms with why this had started and let it all go. I began one by one to tell everyone each day how amazing they were. As I was now less frantic I had the time to give Mum a ring or spend an evening with Phil where I wasn't glued to my laptop.

I could spend time with my girls just having a chat rather than going through my future plans rote fashion. I could just be Mum, be Nicky, be me!

In November I embarked on a girl's holiday with my good friend Deb. We went to my spiritual home, Sedona in Arizona, red rock country. A place full of magic and beauty, with crystal shops on every corner and so much nature and sunshine it always lifted my spirits.

One of my dreams had been to run retreats to this beautiful place and Deb offered to be my 'guinea pig'. So off we went to Heathrow, bags full of all manner of shoe choice, cardigans, necklaces and everything else a girl needs on a road trip! The very nice man on the BA flight kept us topped up with tea and kept Deb company when I dropped off for hours. I had learned my husband's trick of being able to sleep on any flight, which meant the time went quicker – but it wasn't very sociable!

Once in Sedona the magic of the place started to work. When surrounded by such amazing raw, natural beauty relaxation was effortless. As each day went by my inner sentry stood down from his duty, my shoulders dropped several inches and my inner rambler took hold, not worrying about what would tire my body and how far should we walk.

The two of us just explored, we chatted, we giggled. Each morning we would step out in a cardigan and rush back indoors in seconds as the morning freshness of desert life hit us. We decided on a layered look, that went from thick coat and fleece down to strappy t-shirt for the middle of the day, then back to more layers the instant the sun went down again.

I took Deb to each of the energy vortex sites that Sedona is known for. You can read the books and find out about the masculine, feminine or balanced energy of each one, or you can just go and stand to find out for yourself. I always choose the latter, preferring to just be in the moment and see what happens.

On 11th November, 2011, or 11.11.11, I performed the Reiki Master Attunement on Deb at Crescent Moon Ranch, sitting at the foot of Cathedral Rock with the beautiful Oak Creek stream bubbling by. This was one of the most magical, peaceful and mind-blowing experiences I think either of us have ever experienced.

In that moment I felt connected to everyone and everything, I felt myself – the real me, someone who had been missing for a long while. This version of me had been coming back in fits and starts, but in that moment it felt okay for her to step back in completely. Like enticing a frightened rabbit out of its burrow, I could feel my natural self stepping into that sunlit, peaceful November morning as if waking from a deep and peaceful slumber asking, "What have I missed?"

The rest of the day was a bit of a blur – I think it is possible to overdose on hippy vibrations! We wandered around the streets not really shopping and eventually stopped for ice-cream. We were both unable to talk about what had just happened. It wasn't that we didn't have the words – neither of us were known for being tongue-tied! It was just that we were happy to have been there and experienced it, nothing needed to be said.

We had an amazing week, with a trip to the Grand Canyon that Deb had arranged as a thank you for the Reiki Attunement. I had always wondered about a visit to the canyon, but it wasn't top of my list...until I stood at the rim of that 10 mile wide, snow covered expanse of rock in a rainbow of shades and just went, "Wow!"

I was in total awe of the place from that moment on, wandering around and around to get one hundred different pictures from all sorts of angles. Watching an eagle soar overhead gliding on the thermals took my breath away and I had a great conversation with a raven sitting on a roof of an outbuilding.

The vastness. The raw beauty. The colour. The timelessness. It struck me that we humans, with our lists and striving and responsibilities and plans…we forget that we are part of something so much bigger. Not just on our world, but as part of the cosmos.

We get so tied up in worries and everyday stuff that feels like the most important thing in that moment. Yet standing in this place, with ten miles of pure space ahead of me that formed a gaping hole in our planet, everything just seemed so inconsequential. Surely there was a bigger plan, a reason for our being here that was so much more than the minutiae of life that we trap ourselves with every day?

14 OPERATION GODDESS

January 2012 roared in after a very nice Christmas with the family. I often marvelled at how well we all got on together, social times were always easy with our bunch and add a Christmas tree – despite Phil's "Bah Humbug!" comment or two – and things got even better.

We had closed The Witches Brew over the festive period as we figured it wouldn't be a coffee that folks would be craving! So we had good food, good wine and a real chance to relax.

January always brings with it a flurry of resolutions that may possibly endure a week or two before we give up and go back to our old ways. There is something about the clock ticking over into a 365 day period that sends us reaching for a pen and a goal or two.

While pondering the start of the year it had to be said that I was feeling pretty good. I had the odd achy day here and there but generally I was mostly pain free. I still took medication but my blood pressure was mostly under control these days. My left arm was still weaker and my hand stiff if I wrote too much or tried to lift boxes, but I didn't really pay much attention.

Yet I couldn't help wondering: what would be better than this?

It felt as if I would be settling if I stayed where I was. I had made a few dietary changes but still ate a fair proportion of rubbish food and it had started to feel rubbish when I ate it too.

I still had a penchant for red wine and although I could easily go days at a time without a drink, the nights where we drained a bottle and sometimes two between us were rather regular.

My lungs still complained when I did any kind of prolonged walking and I had forgotten how to run! My balance wasn't the best either – not what you would expect after years of ballet training.

I decided to start Operation Goddess!

This would be my own version of a fitness regime, not a quick start and quick fail faddy thing, but rather small changes, an incremental and enduring theme that would run throughout the year. I would look at the food I ate, the amount of water I drank, the exercise I did. I would re-vamp my wardrobe, change my skin care routine and add as much nurture and love of myself as I could each and every day. I wouldn't have an end goal – I would see where I ended up!

This felt good. It felt like the start of something positive and the mystery of not knowing where it would end appealed to my Piscean nature that loved a good adventure. It also felt like taking my own life into my hands, something that had been taken from me by my accident and the onslaught of medical advice and tests of recent years. I was doing this on my own terms, for me.

My first step was to look at the food I ate. I would tell everyone I met to 'eat the rainbow', in other words include fruit and vegetables that were the colours of the rainbow. I loved to do this…but had just forgotten to. It was so much easier to let Phil do the shopping and cooking and get the things he liked – and anyone who knows my husband knows he's very much vegetable averse!

That said he loves certain vegetables, like chillies, onions, peppers and mushrooms so we started there. Through the week he would make amazing winter soups spiced with chilli and ginger. They were low calorie and high taste.

A big tick for Operation Goddess!

Then on to breakfast. I hate breakfast. Any kind. I am never hungry first thing, have a bit of a battle with gluten and dairy which negates cereals or toast…and I just don't think to eat until 11am.

My daughter Kassi had a Nutri Bullet and was always going on about how easy it was to make smoothies, so I thought I would give it a whirl. My first few were a bit tasteless and far too green, but with a bit of experimenting I soon had my favourite, with cucumber and celery, an apple and some coconut water – easy! Of course I had to force myself to the shop a couple of times a week for supplies, but it was pretty straight forward and once I was in the swing it just seemed to happen every day.

Another tick.

Now for the exercise. In the autumn a friend and I had booked a few sessions with a local personal trainer called Dean. He was an ex marine whose reputation went before him – but we had survived, just!

I longed for physical strength, for the confidence to break into a run or lift something without worrying what would happen when I failed. I had mentally become someone with a weak body and it didn't feel right. With everything I had read I knew I could change anything, but perhaps I needed someone on my side to coach me a little.

Soon enough our first session arrived. I had decided to jump right in and do two sessions a week, at 6.30 in the morning when no-one was around. If I was going to get back into lycra the last thing I wanted was an audience, right?

Filling in the medical forms took a while and I'm sure I saw Dean raise an eyebrow as he read my history. He didn't look scared though and listened patiently as I listed all of my protests, couldn't and wouldn't do's.

Those first few sessions were a journey for both of us as I saw my fitness improve week on week and Dean realised with a challenge or a dare I would do more. There were a few odd moments, like the step routine that ended with me falling off as my left and right brain co-ordination didn't exist any more! Also my left arm refused to lift the same as my right…try as I might to visualise that weight in the air nothing would happen.

It seemed I may need another lesson in patience!

Gradually though, with a good diet and exercise I noticed a few changes. I had more energy for a start – I no longer craved an afternoon nap and felt more mentally alert. My muscles became more defined and my breathing improved.

My body really took to the new diet and on days when I slipped I really noticed the difference. I was much more aware of every choice I made when shopping and eating. That phrase, "Garbage in, garbage out" came to mind as I realised I couldn't expect my body to be fit and full of energy when I was feeding it bland, processed, quick fix food. The more smoothies, soups, salads and healthy snacks I fed myself the better I felt.

Of course I would have snacks, I don't think I'll ever stop craving a packet of cheese and onions crisps and a bar of chocolate! I can however make that the exception rather than the rule.

At the gym the weights I lifted increased and every week I pushed myself further. Soon there was no difference right to left, my balance had got back to my dancer level and I was feeling amazing!

I worked with Dean for 18 months, then choosing then to ease back into a more natural routine of walking and swimming. It felt like the right thing to do, I had woken up my body which initially had felt fragile and confused. I had tested it to its limits and given it a new set of skills, as well as a new neural roadmap of where everything was and what it was supposed to do. I will forever be indebted to Dean for his tact, his encouragement and his humourous phrases that had me bursting into fits of giggles. Getting fit on my own would have been a daunting, arduous and much less interesting task!

I decided that Operation Goddess should be an on-going, continuously improving part of my life. It was easy to sigh and accept when a few pounds crept on, or to tell yourself next week would be better when those bad for you foods appeared magically in the shopping trolley. To tell yourself that it had been a stressful week and you deserved that bottle of wine.

Actually, in essence I feel I am cheating myself when I do this. I am denying myself the glowing health, flexible body and ability to embrace life in an energy full state.

Operation Goddess allows me to maintain the mind-set that says: "What one thing can I do today that my future self will thank me for?" Asking for one thing means it doesn't feel overwhelming, if a little too easy. What this does though is leads to more good choices, regularly, so that the scales are always running in my favour.

So many people accept how they are and when an accident, incident or health challenge comes along they accept it as part of life or part of ageing. What if instead we researched, adapted and grew a mind-set that allowed life to be a continual improvement? An experience that lead to us getting younger and more flexible every day and willing to choose the best outcome, every time? This is my choice.

15 CHANGING TIMES

Through my newly found fitness when our annual ski holiday came around in early February I could carry my skis to the slopes without turning bright pink! My confidence increased further as my legs did as they were told and I really enjoyed my new ability level.

We had picked Soldeu in Andorra for this year's trip and it was nice to embrace the full on, jump on the first lift and go for it attitude. Skiing had not come easily to me and it had been a mind over matter battle, first overcoming my fear of heights through hypnotherapy and then learning the basics of a sport where speed is your friend.

I had never been a really sporty person, choosing the serenity of the ballet studio over the frenetic hockey pitch. Emotionally I was fearless, but putting my physical self high on a slippery mountain had taken time to master!

What won me around was the amazing scenery and bracing, fresh air. The glisten of an untouched piste, being kissed by the first morning sun. The banter and friendship that goes with a group holiday – feeling like you were on an expedition, keeping a caring eye on your companions and if they do fall – giggling with them as long as you are sure they're not hurt first!

I felt like life was returning to a normality when my health and strength weren't the first consideration for any activity. I no longer felt like a fragile shell, threatening to break at any moment. I could plan my future in any way I chose and this felt good.

My birthday is in February and I have always loved surprises. No matter how old I get my birthday brings with bags of excitement. I spend weeks reminding everyone, even though I know they have remembered.

For me it has never been the size of the present, but the fact that someone you love took some time to choose something they know you will like. I love to return the favour too, often spotting the perfect gift months before a birthday, but knowing that thing would be perfect for a certain person.

This year the birthday babble started early as I realised my family were in cahoots. There were hushed conversations that stopped when I walked in and Phil could often be seen poring over his laptop clicking away. When I asked what they were doing I got some scrabbled together answer that of course I accepted with a little smile. The suspense was driving me crazy and increasing my excitement – what were they planning!?

A few days before my birthday I received my instructions: pack a weekend case, we're off to Rome! Rome is my favourite city, with its Piazzas, romantic cafes, statues, fountains and wonderful history. I had often told Phil all about it, but never thought we would get to experience it all together!

I couldn't contain my smiles and excitement as we got on our flight. We chinked our champagne glasses and I told Phil for the thousandth time that he was the best husband ever.

Ami and Kassi were left holding the fort at the coffee shop and shooed me away when I tried to list what needed doing. They were naturals at running my business now; at 19 and 21 they took everything in their stride and promised they wouldn't be ringing my mobile to interrupt my fun!

We spent a heavenly few days exploring the city, watching the world go by from outside sunny cafes. Phil really had needed that laptop – he had a full itinerary of where we should go each day, re-visiting some of my favourite spaces and finding some great new locations and restaurants.

The hotel was amazing too – as my birthday cards were on display they speedily arranged for another card and some champagne. I felt like the most spoiled and happy girl in the world, so loved, so looked after and so safe.

Life can so easily pass us by in a frenzy of lists, tasks and obligations, but when we take time out to experience something new it also gives us the time to count every single one of our blessings.

This time last year I had been dragging my foot along the floor. Every day involved a calculation to ensure I had enough energy. I had just been given a label of stroke sufferer that had weighed so heavily around my neck like a sentence and I had wondered whether life would ever be the same again. It turned out it wouldn't be, but with those small initial steps that had felt like leaps so much more continued to be possible.

Once home armed with a thousand pictures and a heart full of love the adventuring continued - it was my turn to do the scheming!

For his birthday in April Mr Marshall was the one to pack a case. I kept the secret all to myself right up until we were on the train heading to St. Pancras – we were off to Paris! This was a city neither of us had visited and so together we explored La Louvre, Le Champs Elysee, Notre Dame, Le Moulin Rouge and many other sights. There was more enjoyment of sunny cafes and exploring – although my itinerary didn't have quite such rigour!

It was amazing spending so much time together. In all our years of going out and marriage we have never crossed words or raised voices. We have had discussions and disagreed, but always with gentleness and respect. The events of recent months had meant our roles had changed so much – my independent streak and stubborn nature had been relegated to the subs bench as I asked Phil for help.

There were times during those midnight hours where I had questioned why Phil would want such a weak and scared rabbit for a wife. Would he continue to love me for who I now was – I didn't want a carer but couldn't ignore the help I needed and the outward signs that inward mental torture leaves. We had both promised to love in sickness and in health but it was a lot to ask!

As we enjoyed our weekends together exploring romantic cities it became apparent that our marriage was stronger than ever. The giggles we shared, the sarcasm and quips, the way Phil would ask out of the blue, "Have I told you how much I love you today?" Every minute we were together was easy, relaxed and fun. How blessed was I to be able to share my experiences with this amazing man?

When the new dive season started I was feeling much more robust - mentally, physically and spiritually. I wanted to take more of a part in trips, even if I could only drive. My problem was that although my strength was much improved I wouldn't be able to lift the heavy kit back into the boat when the divers surfaced.

Once more Phil came to the rescue! A series of clips meant each diver could take their kit off and clip it to the boat, climb in and then haul their own kit in, voila! I named these clips my 'crip handles', once again making light out of my situation. It allowed me to view those handles as my ticket to be part of the trip, rather than a reminder of what I couldn't do.

I now felt part of the sport that I loved again, rather than it being something that had been taken away from me. I loved diving because it was out in nature, peaceful and in touch with the sea. When all the divers were underwater I would sit at the helm – still out in nature, still peaceful and totally in touch with the sea.

Of course I knew it wasn't the same, but the universe had come up with a really good second best and for this I was grateful.

It was after one such diving weekend that everything changed, again. This particular Monday I walked into the coffee shop to find Ami sitting at our admin desk at the far end of the shop. As I walked in she lifted her head from her laptop as she had done countless times before. This time however, just before she grinned to greet me I noticed something: she was tired.

Not just a 'had a busy weekend and could do with some sleep' tired, but an 'I'm bored of this' tired. In those seconds as I looked at Ami I realised something else: I was also tired. Again, not in a physical way – but the dream business I had created was now a weight around my neck. It dawned on me that I had accepted the tiredness of late as part of my recovery and yes, to a point it was. The tiredness was also a message that I needed to do something different.

"We're done." I said simply.
"What do you mean?" Ami replied.

"Look me in the eye and tell me you still love what we do here?" I said, "Honestly, 100 percent."

Ami made that face that told me everything. There was so much still to love about what we did, but the constant routines, the checklists for health and safety, the endless promotion and marketing…it had become too much and we hadn't noticed.

I realised now I had stopped to actually think about it that my time was so full of managing staff, managing therapists and running the business that I hardly saw any of my own clients any more. The reason for the business was helping people and it was – but in that moment I wanted to do more of the helping.

I had thought starting a business was a big and scary task, but I now realised that selling a business was worse! I toyed with the thought of closing the doors, terminating the lease and emptying the shop – the path of least resistance right?

I allowed myself to sit with this for a while. The old me was one for a snap decision, but recent events had shown me what time and determination could do. What if however, there was someone out there who wanted to run a coffee shop? What if I could sell for a profit? And what if this was just a blip in my energy and I was actually supposed to keep going?

After hours of discussion and research I decided to put the shop on the market with a local agent. If I was supposed to do something different it would sell easily and if I wasn't…well, it wouldn't! On Friday afternoon we officially went on the market. I had butterflies and questions but gave everything up to the universe, saying aloud often, "What will be, will be!"

On Tuesday we had an offer and by the following Friday the legalities started – you could say that was a sign I was supposed to move on! After a few months of writing stock lists, furniture lists and handing over procedures along with a legal delay or two and many a moment taking deep breaths we handed over the keys to The Witches Brew on November 2nd.

It felt very strange doing this. I had so many memories of our time in Whitchurch, the actual reality of a decade of dreaming. The shop was a place where we had turned an unloved, disused shell crumbling before our eyes into a modern, nurtured and welcoming space where coffee was made, cake and paninis consumed and friendships were formed.

There had been more smiles of course, but a few tears too and of course if I hadn't set off on this path there may not have been a diving accident and stroke that changed everything forever.

I would not have signed up for the painful bits and had many a moment of why the blazes did this happen to me, but the way I was living now was an upgraded and improved version of life before. I took nothing for granted, I made the most of every day and I counted my blessings with a big smile on my face.

I also realised I was a very good businessperson. My skills now included health and safety, food hygiene, organising an army of staff and therapists as well as playing Maître D', problem solving, networking and lastly sharing our whole story on social media so even strangers felt they were part of our story (which of course, they were).

Would I have gone ahead if I had known how much work and effort was involved? Probably not. Did I regret my choices – never! As they say life gives us what we need and not what we want and now I had a treasure chest of memories to box up and a new chapter to begin.

We decided to rent a small, ready to go space in Keynsham just ten minutes from home and offer therapies and workshops. It was just Ami and myself, sharing therapy and office space. Compared to our coffee shop tasks days were much simpler and we both welcomed our new roles.

As 2012 drew to a close there were two themes running through my ever-enquiring brain. It seemed normal to me that I was forever questioning, wondering if I was on the right path and doing the right thing. According to Phil I am an exception to the rule and not everyone did this…which was a surprise!

The first theme was around my work. Holistic therapies are great and through treatments people can be pain free, ailments can disappear and watching someone get off the treatment couch with a big smile was amazing to be a part of.

However people relied on me as a therapist to make this happen and often made no other changes to reduce the cause of the stress that caused the problem in the first place.

I knew from personal experience how many changes I had made to get better, but also I now had a great sense of owning my health. I knew that many conditions could be alleviated or even eliminated with changes to lifestyle and mind-set. I wanted everyone to feel that personal power, to maybe include therapies, but as a wider, holistic plan for their mind, body and spirit.

I was looking for a deeper meaning, a more permanent solution for the people that came for treatment and relief from their stress. It was lurking in the depths of my brain, floating around just out of view. I knew that once it came into full view a new branch to my work would take flight.

The second theme came up to be heard and was squashed many times before I allowed it too much head space. This second thought took me back into my own story and would require big girl pants and that stubborn streak of mine. I didn't want to give this thought too much space and excitement as the answer may simply be no and may need to be silenced forever.

On New Year's Eve after a few glasses of wine this thought blurted out, along with a stream of tears that took a while to stem, "I really want to dive. I miss it and I can't accept that I'll never get in the water again." There, it was out and now I had another step to take.

16 THE DIVER RETURNS

As usual Phil was pragmatic, calm and logical. If he was surprised he didn't show it, instead chatting through a very sensible plan. Helen, the GP who had been on Lundy that day was also a diving referee and would be responsible for signing me off as fit to dive. He suggested dropping her a line to ask what the next steps would be.

After a few e-mails I had my answer. As my blood pressure was now stable and regulated by a small dose of medication and I had no more tingling or numbness in my arm and leg then she would be happy to sign me off.

So that was it, I was ready to dive again. I realised that without all the various treatments and personal training my limbs could still be numb or tingling. Without my dietary changes, stress reduction and mind-set change my blood pressure could still be raging. All the while I had been trying to get better, not knowing if this was possible or where I would end up I was getting ever closer to this day.

When the neurologist had said how I was in 18 months was how I would be forever and that I would never dive again I could have taken him at his word. I could have accepted the status quo, not lifted a finger and this day would have never come.

Amazing what a stubborn streak can do, I thought.

So here I was, able to dive any time I liked. Now I had the green light I felt a little rooted to the spot, was this really what I wanted to do? My family had watched me go through so much, how would they feel while I was off on a dive weekend?

As usual rather than get overwhelmed by the big picture I decided to just head to the swimming pool and see how it felt being under a small amount of water first!

Now I had to assemble some kit as I had sold all of mine when I thought my diving days were over. Ami had a tiny jacket, Phil had spare cylinders and regulators and I still had a wetsuit, boots and fins in the hope that I could at least snorkel…it wasn't as slick as my own kit had been but it would do.

I was surprised at how easily I put my kit together, it seemed those years of drills had paid off and soon Phil and I were stood neck deep in the pool. "I'll wait for you, in your own time." He said, probably due to the slightly panicked look on my face. He couldn't hear my pounding heart or hear the "What the f*%$ are you doing?" that my brain was yelling. Every cell I had was on red alert and I questioned what my blood pressure would read at this moment. We have this innate sense of avoiding anything that can harm us and right now my sense was at its peak. Flashes of murky depths, coastguards and recompression chambers sped through my wired brain.

After what seemed an age I managed to replace those images with sunny days out on boats, or pretty fish and imposing wrecks majestically gracing the sea bed. I took deep, calm breaths, put my regulator in my mouth and dropped to my knees. There, I was in.

We spent a playful half hour under water and I wasn't the awkward duckling I thought I would be. My buoyancy was if anything better than before and we went through all the drills of removing and replacing masks, lifting each other to the surface and swapping regulators in case our air ran out. One minute it seemed like I had never been away and the next I felt like pinching myself, unable to believe I was back in the water.

We booked a trip to Tenerife in June, with Geoff who had taught me PADI Advanced Diver all those years ago. He sent a very lovely e-mail back, thrilled that I would be joining him again and assuring me I would be looked after. With an instructor for a husband and Geoff too I felt very safe at this point.

So this was it, I was going to dive again. This time I would give myself some ground rules. As I had discovered it's very easy to plan a holiday and then squeeze in as much as you can before you go. It's easy to talk yourself into every dive going without a thought for your health and energy. Some people say it's peer pressure, but I think it's the pressure we put on ourselves. We have choices and can make really good ones, with a little time, thought and gut instinct.

To satisfy myself and also to stop my family worrying I decided I would dive three out of the seven days and only the shallower, afternoon dives. I would ensure I drank plenty of water, rested after the dives and give myself plenty of preparation time before we went, finishing a day earlier than my usual drop everything and run routine!

In the months after my bend I had crazy dreams of being stuck in the weed in the murky depths of the ocean, unable to escape and gasping for breath. As our holiday came closer they returned, along with dreams of being lost on huge boats, unable to find my kit and of Phil going in with other groups leaving me all alone. By day I was excited at the thought of diving again, but I had to admit my subconscious had some very big concerns. When I sat with my hands on my tummy and really thought about diving, I got a very strong sense of it being right. I was going, but I would keep checking in just in case.

Tenerife is a beautiful island that has welcomed tourism and every year new hotels and amenities are added. The people are lovely and vibrant, beautiful flowers and lush lawns abound. It has always felt like home, so diving here was a pleasure. Being a volcanic island the underwater topography is striking and dramatic.

Again I had a moment. All kitted up and ready to go, fins on, regulator in mouth and jacket inflated ready to roll backwards into the water...I froze. I took my regulator out, took a few deep breaths and made a joke - choosing to mock myself, as I know a laugh will break my own tension.

I had a little word, put my regulator back in and with a quick okay signal rolled backwards before I could stop and think again. As I descended the shot line down to the anchor I knew I was breathing too fast and that my air wouldn't last for a long dive if I carried on. So I began spotting fish:

Parrot Fish, Blennies, Spider Crabs and those pesky black Urchins waiting to spike a finger or knee. Soon my breathing was back to a slow and steady pace and I had a great reminder of why I dive!

On our second day of diving the mind monkeys won a victory. I had been out on the boat in the morning helping Phil and the others to kit up and enjoying the sunshine. After a nice lunch it was time to head back to the boat for my dive. On the way the mind chatter started...I think I feel a bit sick, perhaps I have sunstroke? Maybe I am dehydrated; it would be bad to dive in that state with your history wouldn't it? I think the wind has got up, if it's choppy you know you'll be seasick don't you?

By the time we were half way there I had convinced myself I wouldn't be diving and ignored Phil's concerned looks. I subsequently sat with a coffee crossly chastising my mind monkeys as the boat pulled away full of happy divers. No matter how much time passed I concluded I would have a groove in the record of my memory and now and again, it would surface. I had to let this be okay and let go of the frustrations that once were so raw. In time, this too would pass and one day I would be monkey free.

Our last day's diving passed without issue and I marvelled at how well I controlled my air (lots of meditation and breathing exercises) and how much less lead on my weight belt I needed to sink (less fat more muscle, hurrah!). I decided to leave cold water, UK diving for now while I got used to everything and I really wasn't sure I would ever want to peel that rubber over my head and hair to get into a dry suit again! There was, however, a live aboard trip to Egypt happening in December and Phil and I booked up.

Egypt had always been a favourite diving destination of ours, with its stunning sea life and beautiful coloured corals of every shape and size. The water is so warm and you can see even further than in Tenerife.

The guides give very good briefings of the reefs and wrecks and each day you feel like you are heading out on adventure as there is always a chance sighting of a shark or dolphin to be had. One year a Green Turtle hitched a ride with Phil, spending 20 minutes hanging on to his shoulder, every so often looking into his mask as if to say, "Okay if I stay a while longer mate?" It's this kind of memory that will get talked about for years to come and each trip brings more.

I had never stayed on a live aboard boat before but quickly got to see why it's so popular. You creep on deck for an early cup of tea to take back to the cabin, or hop in the water for a pre-breakfast dive. There are further dives mid morning and mid afternoon plus a night dive and you can choose as many or as few as you like.

Our dive guide Becky was amazing once I told my story. Each day as she did the brief she would give me a sneaky thumbs up and thumbs down and so I could quietly choose my dives. Most days I did the mid-morning dive, then choosing to 'rest' after my dive on the sunny top deck with a cup of tea and a book.

My action man husband jumped in the water at least three, if not four times a day and would report back tall tales of Spanish treasure and mermaids.

There was one dive I knew I had to do. SS Thistlegorm was a steam ship used in the second world war, when she got stuck in Egyptian waters unable to pass through the Suez Canal. German intelligence was that there was a ship carrying a large number of troops and chose the Thistlegorm as she was so low in the water.

Rather than troops, the Thistlegorm mostly carried Bedford trucks, armoured vehicles, motor cycles and Bren guns, as well as ammunition, wellington boots and two locomotive steam engines. Sadly 9 people lost their lives that day, but the death toll could have been so much worse.

For the modern day diver, this means there are three levels of in tact ship to explore full of treasure, as well as the bounty of wildlife that live there. I had loved my first dive on her in my early years and this was the dive that I had felt the saddest about never doing again.

Mid-week with Becky as my buddy we descended into the deep blue waters of the Thistlegorm. For the next 45 minutes we explored the upper decks and found Crocodile fish, bright blue Fusiliers, Nudibranchs, Lionfish and a host of other sea life. We weaved our way in and out of the wreck, visited one of the locomotives that had been blown sideways onto the seabed and generally had a darn good rummage.

Coming up the shot line looking back at this majestic wreck there were salty tears stinging my eyes as I marvelled at this experience. Some may wonder what all the fuss is about, but diving is a magical experience where you see sights few others see. There is a camaraderie and an understanding that I felt was lost to me and yet here I was.

Life is a pretty amazing cacophony of twists and turns, unexpected developments and moments that take our breath away. In a blink of an eye or a heartbeat everything can change, in good ways and in bad and amongst this chaos we get to love, to experience and to learn about everything life has to offer. I had no idea what the future would hold, but I intended to snapshot and appreciate every single moment.

ACT TWO

INTRODUCTION

I have thought long and hard about writing this book and taken my time getting it to a place where I'm happy with it. Over the years I have written blogs, Facebook posts, keynote speeches and meditations and I know people have enjoyed them, but there is always that little negative voice sitting on my shoulder saying, "But who would want to read your story?". I think most of us have that voice, nagging us to play small and not make waves…so this book is a bit of a tsunami, ha ha!

I did wonder whether to write Act Two at all, to instead just share my back to diving story and leave it at that. I have always had this quest to help others though and this second act may just help one person, or it may help quite a few…so I thought I would add it in as a gift in the hope of someone doing something better as a result of my writing.

17 DEAR READER

From the desk of Nicky Marshall, St Mary's, Isles of Scilly (the current Bounce HQ) September 2016

Yesterday I completed my first dive in UK waters for over six years. I chose my more comfortable, if a little chilly wetsuit for this and had great fun exploring the wrecks of the Plympton and Hathor at 25 metres. It felt like closure, being back in UK waters where my story began in July 2010.

My buddies and the rest of the group were great, keeping an eye on me and checking whether I was nervous. Actually I wasn't, which felt rather good. In diving and in life I have changed. A lot. I now choose to do the things that intuitively feel right to me. I choose my limits and do my own thing, my way.

Does that sound selfish to you? It would have to the old me, but I have come to realise that if you are high energy and full of health you can help and influence so many more people.

Have you ever been asked to do something and as you said yes felt an inner groan or sigh? You know that really you should say no as you are already tired or overwhelmed? I never get that now as I choose to say yes or no according to my health, energy and time. I willingly help as many people as I can, as I always nurture myself first. I am blessed to teach this and many other tips and techniques as a result of the questioning of my work back in December 2012.

Discover Your Bounce was born in April 2013 over three, 3am sessions.

What we also need is intuition. We need to reassure ourselves or speak to someone that will soothe us. We need human touch, a hug or someone to take our hand. We need to focus on a positive outcome and take steps every day to work towards that goal. We may not see instant results, but it's okay to be not okay…for a while.

Sometimes an illness or injury allows us to step back from busy, to re-assess our life and circumstances. Often it's only a small change that is required to bring back balance and health.

My wish is that people don't wait until they have the chaos of that. With small, easy choices of good diet, enjoyable exercise and positive thinking techniques we could all stay happy. We can remember that we work to live and don't exist just to work. We can remember to add in some fun even on the busiest of days. We can check in with ourselves daily and ask, "How are you doing?"

By all means enjoy a therapy, work with a mentor or coach and accept orthodox medicines when they are needed.

But please, Dear Reader, know that it is your choices that control where you end up. Your daily habits and routines that build your energy. Your right to a happy, healthy and fulfilled life that will give you the courage to find a better way. Other people can help and advise, but when we take control of our own destiny and trust our choices – that is when the magic happens!

It's so easy at a low ebb to give away our power. To a spouse, a parent, a doctor, a coach. We then start losing our identity, our energy and resolve, it drains away drip by drip until we feel totally lost and overwhelmed.

If you feel this has happened to you - stop. Take a breath. Acknowledge what has happened and know that you made the best decisions you could with the knowledge and skills you had at that time. Now say to yourself, as many times as you need, "Today, I am taking my power back."

Over the next few days make as many decisions as you can. Say no to things you would normally say yes to and vice versa. Change the colour of clothes you wear, vary your route to work. Clean your teeth with the opposite hand (this one can be very frustrating but go with it!)

Look for signs that your power is back. People will ask if that's a new dress or suit. They will ask if you have had your hair cut/lost weight/been on holiday. This is because they know something is different but they can't quite work out what.

Once you are feeling more powerful build a routine of good habits – good food, good exercise and personal development. Over the years I have been inspired by countless great people who have assured me that I too can change. When we read the stories of others we know that we can change our circumstances. It spurs us on to take that first step.

I have seen many people who embark on a huge change routine, whether it's a new job, new project, or new house…all without boosting their energy first.

They may achieve their goal, but ultimately their health suffers or some kind of calamity comes along soon after. When you fill yourself up, boost your energy and build good health first, projects flow more easily and your own equilibrium remains. I dived head first into The Witches Brew on a diet of coffee and cake, a cocktail of no sleep and huge action with a sprinkling of panic and fear…you've read my book now, you know where that got me!

Operation Goddess is still running today, not in such a big way but every day I try to challenge myself to make a positive change. My cholesterol is down from 6.6 to 4.9 and I credit Mr. Fruit and Mrs. Vegetable with this progress! I know that if I want to make a change to my health it's possible and this is a good place to be!

I have written this book from a variety of places around the world and although some of my business is based in Bristol our online programme means I can work anywhere I choose. I have come to understand that for my own peace I need a balance of alone time and being with others, so I work my week accordingly.

I am a morning person, so may be at my desk at 6am or attending an early morning networking session, but I rarely work an evening and I'm in bed by 10pm (or earlier) most evenings.

I still have a busy brain, but channel that into writing, or choose a meditation to bring in some silence. I still have a few pounds to lose and could be fitter, but I choose something every day my body will thank me for. I still have days where I lose my confidence, or feel overwhelmed with the global mission I've chosen…but I allow myself to be human, take days to nurture myself and freely admit when I get it wrong.

My hope is that you will read this book and see how a fellow human being went on an adventure after adversity and found a place they like. I hope that you will take a look at where you are now and feel blessed and grateful for all the good bits. If there are any changes to make I hope you will do this from a loving place, choosing gradual, peaceful steps…but please choose those steps.

My heart sinks when I hear people tell me all the medications they are on and the side effects they suffer, without a thought that they could do something different. Or when someone has accepted a label given to them by another and believes that they are dumb, ugly or useless. I get so sad when I see a beautiful soul suffering.

When we take steps to improve our own life we never know who we are encouraging. By being the highest and best version of yourself you give others permission and the inspiration to do the same. We may never find out the impact we had, but that's okay.

So, Dear Reader, end this book and start your own journey. Ask yourself what would be totally brilliant if it happened to you and then take a step or two to make it happen. I would love you to let me know your triumphs, but if not then just know that I am proud of you for getting up today, for taking a breath and making a difference. I thank you for joining me on my journey and wish you a wonderful future full of toe curling happiness.

CREDITS

I would like to thank the Devon Coastguard and the Diver Diseases Research Centre in Plymouth for their care and attention in my hour of need.

Writing about this time with the benefit of hindsight I can of course appreciate and acknowledge the amazing work that these people do. Every day they have the possibility of facing a life threatening situation for someone at sea and act with speed and efficiency while also taking the time to care. They stepped in willingly and I am so grateful that they did.

It troubles me that I can't remember their names or recall a clear memory of their faces – something in normal life I am famous for. Names sometimes elude me but I can always recall the scenario of where I have met someone and usually even what they were wearing. At that point however I was in the midst of a chemical reaction, the magnitude of which I was only beginning to realise.

I would also like to thank the experts that helped me with my holistic recovery. Complementary therapy is just that – an addition to orthodox medicine, but the wealth of knowledge about the body that you can gain from people trained in this field is amazing and can give you the insights you need and give the body the energy to begin to self heal. The people below took me into their care and gave me the respite and peace from my symptoms that I needed to regain some clarity and balance.

Huge thanks go to:

Ami Marshall – no longer practicing therapies but still using her wisdom!

Jemima Price – www.crystals-online.co.uk

Jeni Briggs – www.thecourtyardosteopaths.co.uk

Louise Alley – www.integratedhealth.support

Louise Morgan – www.louise-morgan.co.uk

Mary English – www.maryenglish.co.uk

ACKNOWLEDGEMENTS

Cover Design: Laura Barnett

Cover Photo: Kirsty Andrews

Back Cover Artwork: Hayley Rust – www.therustyunicorn.com

Thanks also to Marsha Wright for her beautiful foreword that gave me both tears and goose bumps when I read it. This lady asked me some questions that totally changed my business direction and for that I will be eternally grateful.

Thanks also to my army of wonderful proof readers and to Laura, Ami and Chris who burned the midnight oil to make this book happen to schedule!

RESOURCES AND FURTHER READING

How Your Mind Can Heal Your Body – Dr David Hamilton

Flip It – Michael Heppell

Infinite Resources – Mike Dooley

DISCLAIMER

ABOUT THE AUTHOR

Nicky has a unique talent for breaking down the barriers that hold you back in life and giving you the confidence, energy and passion to live the life of your dreams.

After suffering a stroke and fully recovering within 3 years, Nicky walks her talk and can hold your hand through your 'bouncing back' process. She has 11 books in publication with more in the pipeline. She hosts retreats and regular events, she's a speaker and a mentor – so pick your method for change!

Nicky has passion in buckets, she loves to inspire, she gives great hugs and she's a good listener. She can give you a stern pep talk or hold your hand through any process. Nicky's knowledge, knack for stress-busting and infectious laugh is a favourite combination with her many clients and audiences.

Follow these links to connect with Nicky:

www.discoveryourbounce.com

www.facebook.com/discoveryourbounce

www.facebook.com/nickymarshallauthor

www.twitter.com/bounce2success

https://www.youtube.com/channel/UCBXK2Ut7IyL39-Pc1cRr2lA

Or send her an e-mail: nicky@discoveryourbounce.com

ARE YOU READY TO DISCOVER YOUR BOUNCE?

Discover Your Bounce Online – Life Coaching and Mentoring from home.

A six-part course from the comfort of your own home, helping you become happier, healthier, and more energised; giving you the confidence and drive to create your own future.

Written by Nicky, Discover Your Bounce online is a six-part course that you can work through from your own home in your own time. The course is specifically designed to help change your thinking, routines and future vision, resulting in a healthier, more positive outlook. The course will focus on a different part of your life each week, helping you look at decision making, ways of thinking, nurturing routines and visualisations to work towards your goals.

The course will help you achieve the following:

Increased energy: By removing negativity, distancing yourself from aspects of life that drain you, and re-focusing your mind your energy levels will quickly increase. This will allow you to spend more time on the things that inspire you and make you happy.

Clarity: Working out what you want to achieve, and what path you want your life to take can be one of the most difficult things to overcome. When life events seem to have clouded your judgement it can be difficult to find clarity. The course will work to help you decide what direction you want to take and the best way to achieve this.

Life organisation: Everyone's lives are full of obstacles – whether they are physical or emotional. The course will recommend practical exercises to help you overcome and even leave behind these obstacles – whether it be memories from a difficult time, or a cluttered house that you haven't had the energy to tidy, using some simple activities and visualisations the course will help your life become clear and calm.

A life that you love: Whether it is general health, fitness, your career path, weight loss or even just feeling happy when you wake up in the morning, this course is designed for you to discover your bounce and enjoy life every day, no matter what you are looking to achieve.

A note from Nicky:

"After experiencing my share of misfortunes, from a messy divorce, depression and anxiety to suffering a stroke at 40, I decided it was time for change. During that time, I spent years learning everything I could to be fitter, healthier and to create a business I love. I've spent thousands of hours and pounds learning from experts and gurus through books, workshops and programs, which have allowed me to live the amazing life I do today. I managed to turn my life around and now I am passionate about helping others to do the same in a way that is easy and fun!

If this program isn't for you then I urge you to at least do *something* – because nothing will change until you do."

Choose to invest in yourself today! Sign up at www.discoveryourbounce.com/online.

Questions? Message nicky@discoveryourbounce.com.

The End ☺

Printed in Great Britain
by Amazon